A BISHOP AND HIS PRIESTS
TOGETHER

Resources for Building More Intentional Presbyterates

Also by J. Ronald Knott

An Encouraging Word: Renewed Hearts, Renewed Church
The Crossroads Publishing Co., 1995 *(out of print)*

One Heart at a Time: Renewing the Church in the New Millennium
Sophronismos Press, 1999

Sunday Nights: Encouraging Words for Young Adults
Sophronismos Press, 2000

Diocesan Priests in the Archdiocese of Louisville
Archdiocese of Louisville Vocation Office, 2001

Religious Communities in the Archdiocese of Louisville
Archdiocese of Louisville Vocation Office, 2002

For The Record: Encouraging Words for Ordinary Catholics
Sophronismos Press, 2003

Intentional Presbyterates: Claiming Our Common Sense of Purpose as Diocesan Priests
Sophronismos Press, 2003

For The Record II: More Encouraging Words for Ordinary Catholics
Sophronismos Press, 2004

From Seminarian to Diocesan Priest: Managing a Successful Transition
Sophronismos Press, 2004

For The Record III: Still More Encouraging Words for Ordinary Catholics
Sophronismos Press, 2005

For The Record IV: Even More Encouraging Words for Ordinary Catholics
Sophronismos Press, 2006

The Spiritual Leadership of a Parish Priest: On Being Good and Good At It
Sophronismos Press, 2007

Intentional Presbyterates: The Workbook
Sophronismos Press, 2007

For The Record V: Yet More Encouraging Words for Ordinary Catholics
Sophronismos Press, 2007

For The Record VI: Still Yet More Encouraging Words for Ordinary Catholics
Sophronismos Press, 2008

For The Record VII: Even Still More Encouraging Words for Ordinary Catholics
Sophronismos Press, 2009

For The Record VIII: Ongoing Encouraging Words for Ordinary Catholics
Sophronismos Press, 2010

Copies of Father Knott's books can be ordered via e-mail by sending a request to: scholarshop@saintmeinrad.edu.

A BISHOP AND HIS PRIESTS TOGETHER

Resources for Building More Intentional Presbyterates

Rev. J. Ronald Knott, Editor

Sophronismos Press ◆ Louisville, Kentucky

A BISHOP AND HIS PRIESTS TOGETHER
Resources for Building More Intentional Presbyterates

Copyright © 2011 by J. Ronald Knott
All rights reserved.

No part of this book may be used or reproduced in any manner whatsoever without permission except in the case of brief quotations embodied in critical articles or reviews. For information address Sophronismos Press, 1271 Parkway Gardens Court #106, Louisville, Kentucky 40217.

Cover design: J. Ronald Knott
Book layout and design: Lori Massey

First Printing: April 2011
ISBN 978-0-9800023-4-8

Printed in the United States by Morris Publishing®
3212 East Highway 30
Kearney, NE 68847
1-800-650-7888

This book is dedicated to Archbishop Thomas C. Kelly, O.P., who took the risk of recognizing, trusting, nurturing and unleashing my interest in the subject of the ongoing formation of presbyterates. For the persevering support that he has given me over the last twenty-eight years that I have known him, I am truly grateful.

The ongoing formation of a presbyterate is the deliberate cultivation of the unity of the priests and their bishops.

The Basic Plan for the Ongoing
Formation of Priests
III
USCCB

Acknowledgements

I would like to thank Ms. Lori Massey for formatting and editing these articles into a book, as well as Brother John Glasenapp, OSB, Mr. Joseph Cook and Ms. Lea Ann Osterman for researching materials, for getting reprint permissions and for secretarial assistance. Finally, a special word of thanks goes to The Lilly Endowment for making it possible to distribute this book to the Catholic bishops of the United States, as well as a few bishops in other English-speaking countries.

TABLE OF CONTENTS

Preface: Why Do We Need Intentional Presbyterates? xi
    Rev. J. Ronald Knott

CHAPTER 1: A VISION OF UNITY 1

The Two Arms of the Bishop: Presbyterate and Diaconate 3
    Rev. J. Ronald Knott

The Spiritual Renewal of the American Priesthood:
The Relationship of Bishop and Priest in Ministry 5
    Most Rev. Matthew H. Clark

The Presbyterium of the Diocese 23
    Rev. Gary Coulter

From Neglect to Intention: Taking the "Radical Communitarian
Dimension of Ordained Ministry" Seriously 31
    Rev. J. Ronald Knott

Working Toward Intentional Presbyterates: What Can
Priests, Seminaries, Presbyterates and Bishops Do? 39
    Rev. J. Ronald Knott

Affecting Change in a Presbyterate 53
    Rev. Francis Kelly Scheets, OSC

The Promise of Obedience of Diocesan Priests 67
    A Summary from Pastores Dabo Vobis III, 28

That Other Promise: The Role of Obedience
in Unified Presbyterates 69
    Rev. J. Ronald Knott

CHAPTER 2: THE MINISTRY OF UNITY 73

At Odds with Ourselves 75
    David B. Couturier, OFM Cap

Civil Discourse: Speaking the Truth with Respect 91
    Donald Cardinal Wuerl

The Proper Characteristics of Dialogue 97
    Pope Paul VI

Bridge Building in the Presbyterate 99
    Rev. Paul J. Philibert, OP

CHAPTER 3: SOME TOOLS FOR UNITY 109
All articles in Chapter 3 are by Rev. J. Ronald Knott

Creating a Plan and Putting It Into Action 111

Some Major Insights on Priests and Presbyterates from Church Documents 119

Assembly, Convocation and Retreat Models:

    A. Claiming Our Common Sense of Purpose as Diocesan Priests 127

    B. Honoring the Variety of Gifts Within Our Presbyterate 137

    C. Made Holy by Our Shared Ministry 145

    D. The Asceticism of Dialogue in the Ministry of Unity — Learning to Talk to One Another More Effectively 151

Rite for Renewal of Diaconal (Transitional), Priestly and Episcopal Commitments within a Presbyteral Convocation of Priestly Commitments 157

Prayers 163

Discussion Questions for Various Groups within the Presbyterate 169

CHAPTER 4: VARIOUS ISSUES RELATED TO UNITY .. 173

Formation Ministry and Priesthood in a Time of Change and Renewal 175
Most Rev. Gerald F. Kicanas, STL, Ph.D.

Teaching Spiritual Leadership 189
Rev. J. Ronald Knott

Role of the Bishop in Cultivating and Sustaining a Commitment to Lifelong Learning and Ongoing Formation within the Presbyterate 195
Most Rev. Joseph E. Kurtz, DD

CHAPTER 5: A PARABLE OF UNITY 201

The Rabbi's Gift 203

REFERENCES 205

PREFACE:

WHY DO WE NEED INTENTIONAL PRESBYTERATES?

─────── ☙ ───────

Preface:
Why Do We Need Intentional Presbyterates?

Rev. J. Ronald Knott

A bishop has many responsibilities, and many things claim his attention. Presbyteral unity may not seem to be as pressing, for example, as dealing with individual priests who are problematic, with the distribution and assignment of clergy, or with the recruitment of new candidates. Working for presbyteral unity can slip to a lower end of a list of priorities. In fact, its neglect favors divisions and, ultimately, a number of attendant problems in a diocese.
–Basic Plan for the Ongoing Formation of Priests, III

In spite of the unprecedented challenges and ordeals engulfing the priesthood at the turn of the millennium, the *esprit de corps* long associated with Catholic clergy refuses to buckle. The fraternity holds. As the millennium's first rays of dawn catch the contours of the changing face of priesthood, priests still sense they are members of a mysterious brotherhood that continues to shape their lives and world view. Not only is their pastoral identity grounded in the covenant of ordination, they experience a spiritual bond linking them to priests the world over, indeed priests from ages past and to the priests of ages yet to come."[1]

Even though many of these sentiments may still be true, it might be important to note that these words were written immediately before the recent "sexual abuse scandal" that has engulfed American presbyterates. While there are many good things going on in today's presbyterates, and many of them have long and proud traditions, taking past successes for granted is lethal in today's church. The glue that has held us together in the past is breaking down. Today, more than ever, we must be intentional about our "groupness." "The bond of unity within the presbyterate really needs to be stronger today than ever before ..."[2] What we are looking for is a corporate consciousness, a mission in companionship that will fire and unite not only the presbyterate itself, but also the whole diocesan church.[3]

The Basic Plan for the Ongoing Formation of Priests ends with an observation that I came to on my own. "The corporate sense of priestly identity and mission, although not fully developed in official documents, is clearly emerging as an important direction for the future."[4] A "corporate sense of priestly identity and mission" may not yet be "fully developed," but the need for such a corporate sense is now. A presbyterate with a "corporate sense of priestly identity and mission" does not happen automatically. It must be intentional. Intentional presbyterates must be willed into existence by those individual members who are concerned enough to make the commitment to see that it happens.

(1) Why now? To say that presbyterates across the country are facing a dilemma these days is so much an understatement that it is almost laughable. "Dilemma" is the perfect word for our situation, because "dilemma" means "two horns," one horn being "crisis" and the other horn being "opportunity." Obviously, we have a crisis, but maybe not as obvious is the opportunity we have. Gregg Levoy, in his book *Callings,* writes, "An ordeal may serve the purpose of shaking us loose from our moorings in order to set us up for important changes we can't see or imagine yet."[5]

(2) "An Army of One" may be the U.S. Army's motto, but it could be ours as well. In the ordination rite the priests present each impose hands on the candidate and then gather around the bishop as he prays the principal consecratory prayer. By doing that, we participate in welcoming and celebrate the arrival of a new member into our "intimate sacramental brotherhood." "The rite of the imposition of hands by the bishop and all the priests ... has special significance and merit because it points ... to the fact that the priest cannot act by himself; he acts within the presbyterate becoming a brother of all those who constitute it."[6]

"Yet the reality is that sometimes members of presbyterates are set against one another. They are a house divided rather than a family gathered. Some presbyterates are divided ideologically, camps that vie against one another. Diocesan priests find themselves competing against one another, reluctant to applaud anyone else's work for fear it will take away from theirs. Some priests would rather do anything than join brother priests for prayer or for learning or just for fun."[7] This has never been acceptable and, especially now, it can be lethal to presbyterates.

(3) One of the stated reasons for intentional presbyterates is that it promises a more intense pastoral effectiveness. With our numbers shrinking and our responsibilities growing, when have we needed to work as a team more than now? Since we cannot work much harder, we must work smarter, and the smartest way to work is to be intentional about working as a team. Why should we be surprised that parishes cannot work together, when we priests cannot?

(4) Priest shortage! Priest shortage! All the statistics tell us that healthy contact with priests is the reason most young adults make the move toward answering their call to ordained priesthood. One happy and effective priest can do more to promote vocations to diocesan priesthood than a hundred eye-catching billboards. A team of happy and effective priests can do more to promote vocations to diocesan priesthood than a million dollars' worth of clever TV spots. One of my favorite passages on vocations from Vatican II is this one: "Let him (priest) attract the hearts of young people to the priesthood by his own humble and energetic life, joyfully pursued, and by love for his fellow priests and brotherly collaboration with them."[8] Our best chance for attracting vocations to our way of life is to become more "attractive" individually and as a group. How do we become "attractive?" We become more attractive by being what we say we are: partners with the bishop with a corporate consciousness of being sent, with energetic lives joyfully pursued.

(5) I guess the first time I started thinking about the need for intentional presbyterates was shortly after I was ordained. My first assignment was to work in our "home missions." I was sent as far away from other priests as I could be sent in our diocese. Within five years I was living and working alone in two counties. After a few years down there, I was attending a gathering of priests when one of my fellow priests asked me, after I had introduced myself, "What diocese are you in, Father?" I remember answering, quite irritated, "Yours, Father!"

Today, with more than 25% of our new priests being foreign born, some without families, and many others coming to us as new

Catholics through the RCIA process, we must be more intentional than ever about how we welcome and mentor new members, not just into the priesthood, but into our presbyterates. This calls not just for normal one-on-one mentoring, but for group mentoring. In the "old days" we came into our presbyterate in groups of 10-12 after attending seminary together, often for 12 years. Many are coming to us today one at a time after five years or less of seminary training. Our old ways are no longer adequate. We ignore this new reality to our peril and theirs. I have been asked more than once by seminarians, "Will I be alone?" I usually lie a little, but if I told the truth, the answer would be, in most cases, "Yes, unless you solve the problem for yourself."

(6) St. Paul wrote these words to his fellow missionary, Timothy: "Fan into flame the gift God gave you when I laid hands on you." (I Tim. 1:6) We, priests and presbyterates, are daily bombarded with new information. If we are to incorporate this new information, we must continually revise our maps of reality, and sometimes when enough new information has accumulated we must make major revisions. This process of making revisions, particularly major revisions, is painful, sometimes excruciatingly painful. What happens when we have striven long and hard to develop a working view of the world, a seemingly workable map, and then we are confronted with new information suggesting that the map needs to be redrawn? The painful effort required seems frightening, almost overwhelming. What we do, more often than not, is to ignore the new information. Sadly, when we do that, we expend more energy in defending an outmoded view of the world than would have been required to revise and correct it in the first place.[9]

There is always a part of us that does not want to exert ourselves, that clings to the old and familiar, fearful of any change or effort, desiring comfort at any cost and absence of pain at any price, even if the penalty is ineffectiveness and stagnation.[10]

As presbyterates, we are being called to re-form ourselves by incorporating the new realities that are staring us in the face. For our own sakes, for the sake of the mission we have been given and for the sake of future new members, we are being called as presbyterates to regroup, to recommit and to "fan into flame the gift that God gave us."

(7) There are serious dangers in leaving presbyterates to chance. I find it frightening to observe in other priests and feel within myself that pull to isolate oneself from the chaos of today's presbyterates. One priest called this isolation "going into private practice." We are called by the church to make every effort to avoid living our priesthood in an isolated and subjective way and try to enhance fraternal communion in giving and receiving – from priest to priest – of the warmth of friendship, of affectionate help, of acceptance and fraternal correction.[11]

Sadly, the usual practice is to ordain individuals and then set them loose on the people, without support and accountability, to do ministry however they choose to define it. These "lone rangers" often put themselves and the laity at risk by their destructive and uninformed actions. This is especially true for the youngest. Because ordination is often considered a final state, where nothing more has to be done, his elevation to priesthood is likely to freeze him, if isolated, at his adolescent level of adjustment.[12]

Intentional presbyterates may be our best insurance for keeping the vocations we have. Recent research, led by Dean R. Hoge at Catholic University, found that 10 to 15 percent of priests resigned in the first five years of ministry due to loneliness, feelings of being unappreciated, problems of celibacy and disillusionment.[13]

(8) Without intentional presbyterates, some young priests have latched onto the trappings and forms of priesthood from bygone days for their sense of purpose and security. Instead of creating a new way to be an intimate sacramental brotherhood, one that embraces and promotes the ministry of the laity, they settle for dressing up and trying to reenact some imagined "good old days" when priests knew who they were, lay people stayed in their places and all things were right in the heavens. Equally missing the target are those who are out there "doing their own thing," living a priesthood of "private practice," doing ministry however they choose to define it. Most pathetic of all are those who have dropped out psychologically, merely going through the motions of priesthood.

Those who look back may be looking for the right thing, but looking for it in all the wrong places, just as those who are "doing their own thing" are doing. Both ask too little. What is needed in the priesthood is not a restoration, certainly not more disintegration, but a transformation. Restoration is about trying to return to the past. The disintegration of the present is scary, but even some of it can be good, if it leads to new life and not just more death. Transformation is about the future, about "making old things new." Restoration is about things changing. Transformation is about people changing. Only a "group change of heart" will lead to a true renewal of our presbyterates.

(9) I have heard so much about the predictions of how few priests we will have in 2010 and how we will stretch them to fit our parishes, but nobody seems to be asking my question: "Just what condition do you think these remaining priests will be in when 2010 rolls around?" I am firmly convinced that we will not "get better" by leaving things alone, but through a deliberate and decisive will to do so. I don't think it is inevitable that we degenerate into a small band of old Shakers, but I do believe intentional presbyterates are possible – if we do act decisively, now! It was my dream as a vocation director to collaborate with my fellow priests so as to "fan into flame" the energy and joy we so desperately need to have and project. It is a "must" if more young men are going to be attracted to our way of life. If we don't do this for each other, then we will all be left to take care of ourselves, one "lone ranger" at a time.

(10) Presbyterates today have been described as a "house divided." If presbyteral unity is the goal, then we must intentionally and accurately identify and honestly confront the divisions that impede and imperil our unity. As Abraham Lincoln said, "A house divided against itself cannot stand." There are serious consequences to be faced if these divisions are ignored or left to fester. Once named, they can be addressed. Addressing them prepares the way for a more constructive approach to presbyteral formation.

- *Competition.* Priests, like other men ministering in an American cultural context, find themselves socialized by a pattern of competition and comparison evident in contemporary American culture. This competition and comparison can easily foster division.

- *Different Generations in a Presbyterate.* A single presbyterate can easily contain at least four different "formational generations": (1) pre-Vatican II, (2) pre- and post-Vatican II, (3) post-Vatican

II and (4) a new emergent formational generation. Priests from these generations must work side by side, but often they do so uneasily and sometimes with apparent divisions.

- *Clerical Envy.* Clerical envy has always been with us (cf. John 21:20-22). In a hierarchical structure (which parallels business, the military, or government/politics), one might assume that advancement would be correlative to higher rank, greater responsibility or a bigger paycheck. This is not so in the priesthood. Progress in priestly ministry is measured solely on being a better sacramental sign and doing better the tasks of priestly ministry. When there is a lack of clarity about advancement or its symbols, priests will respond to what they *think* is the presence of such signs in others and the lack in themselves. This is fertile ground for breeding divisions.

- *Lack of Attention from the Bishop.* Bishops have many responsibilities. Even though presbyteral unity is ultimately their responsibility, in reality it can slip to a lower end of a long list of priorities. This neglect favors divisions and, ultimately, spawns a number of problems in a diocese.

- *Varied Backgrounds.* Priests in the past followed a predictable pattern. Candidates now come into the seminary at different points and with varying life and work experiences. Although diversity can be enriching, it makes unity and cohesiveness in the presbyterate more challenging and, in fact, can lead to divisions.

- *Varied Theologies and Spiritualities.* Although our faith is one, it can take a number of expressions in theological forms. The current state of theological pluralism can fracture the ability of priests to talk to each other in a common theological language. Likewise, differences in spiritualities (the practice of the faith) can impede a sense of unity and lead to divisions.

- *Varied Languages, Cultures and Places of Origin.* We have never ceased to be an immigrant country, and this fact has had (and continues to have) an impact on the church. Priests come into presbyterates with different racial, cultural and language backgrounds. Although these differences can be enriching, frequently they create dividing lines and cause divisions.

These divisions have significant consequences. They lead to diminished effectiveness that undermines the utilization of valuable human resources needed to address pressing issues. When these divisions are public, and they usually are, they constitute an anti-sign for the community and discourage those who might feel called to the priesthood. Finally, divisions can shift the focus of priests from a wide-ranging diocesan perspective to an anti-Catholic, narrow, localized emphasis on one's own parish with a resultant parochialism or congregationalism.[14]

(11) Since married men and women cannot be ordained and the quality of lay ministry continues to intensify, the least we can do as a body of priests is to get our act together to serve them well and to work with them as partners in ministry. My sense is that lay people are sick to death of the immaturity, bad service, incompetence and inability to lead coming from some priests. Lay people today expect, and deserve, competent pastors with the ability to elicit from and coordinate the charisms of lay people.

Without a close connection to a presbyterate, priests are left to define ministry however they choose to define it, putting themselves and the laity at risk. This can lead to two extremes: (a) authoritarianism and (b) abdication.

Authoritarianism dismisses the rightful role of others as also responsible for carrying on some part of Christ's work, given to them at baptism. Priests today must remember that when authority is duly exercised, it is done not so much to command as to serve. True power derives from the ability to make other people powerful. In those areas where he is obliged to exercise it, exercising proper authority is a gift to the church.

Abdication of responsibility is equally destructive to the church. Many priests have assumed that encouraging lay ministry means the abdication of their pastoral authority, allowing all manner of craziness to fill the vacuum.

"Those in authority must overcome the temptation to exempt themselves from this responsibility. If they do not exercise this authority, they no longer serve. In close communion with his Bishop and his faithful, the priest should avoid introducing into his pastoral ministry all forms of authoritarianism and forms of democratic administration that are alien to the profound reality of the ministry, for these lead to a secularization of the priest and a clericalization of the laity. Behind such approaches to the ministry there is often a hidden fear of assuming responsibility or naming mistakes, of not being liked or of being unpopular, or, indeed, reluctance to accept the cross."[15]

Priests are called not only to be leaders of the community, but also teachers of the Word and ministers of the sacraments. Many priests have discovered, as well, that the handing over of administrative duties to others does not mean that all of a sudden they are left with extraordinary spiritual leadership skills. It's a lot easier to balance a budget than inspire a congregation to move into a new level of discipleship. As spiritual directors of the community, we must strive not only to be good ourselves, but also to be good at what we do, being good "group spiritual directors" of the congregations entrusted to us.

(12) We need intentional presbyterates, especially now, precisely because, as a group, we are tired. *Reflections on the Morale of Priests*, a 1988 document of the NCCB Committee on Priestly Life and Ministry, made this sad observation: "Among some priests, there is a significant number who have settled for a part-time presence to their priesthood. … They elect to drop out quietly. Many more of our priests believed in renewal, were willing to adapt, worked hard and are now just plain tired."[16]

"I Will Give You Shepherds" warns young priests about the dangers of being tired. "With priests who have just come out of the seminary, a certain sense of "having had enough" is quite understandable when faced with new times for study and meeting. But the idea that priestly formation ends on the day one leaves the seminary is false and dangerous, and needs to be totally rejected."[17]

(13) Finally, assuming we will continue receiving new members into our presbyterates, we need intentional presbyterates for the sake of those who will follow us. The "millennial generation," young adults entering college beginning in 2000, has been characterized as "used to structure," "trusting organizations and authority," "more collegial by experience" and "liking to work together in teams to complete and resolve problems." They assert that the predominant cause of the problems in our culture is "selfishness."[18] A "lone-

ranger" approach to priesthood will not be attractive to this generation. What will be attractive to this new generation of priests will be the "communion with" and the "common sense of purpose" of presbyterates.

I once heard a story about St. Bernard and his monks, who traveled through France on foot. They were so happy and attractive that, when they passed through some towns, parents hid their children out of fear that they would run off and join them. Today some parents hide their children out of fear they will be unhappy if they do join us.

END NOTES

1. Cozzens, Donald B., *The Changing Face of the Priesthood*, The Liturgical Press, Collegeville, MN, 2000, pp. 47, 48.

2. *The Bridge Magazine*, Interview with Bishop Wilton Gregory, University of Saint Mary of the Lake/Mundelein Seminary, Mundelein, IL, Winter 2002/03, p. 3.

3. Aschenbrenner, George A., *Quickening the Fire in Our Midst*, Loyola Press, Chicago, IL, 2002, p. 133.

4. *The Basic Plan for the Ongoing Formation of Priests*, p. 93.

5. Levoy, Gregg, *Callings: Finding and Following an Authentic Life*, Three Rivers Press, New York, NY, 1997, p. 316.

6. *Directory for the Life and Ministry of Priests*, Libreria Editrice Vaticana, Città del Vaticano, 1994, no. 25.

7. Kicanas, Gerald F., "The Heart and Core of Diocesan Priesthood," *Vocation Journal*, National Conference of Diocesan Vocation Directors, Little River, SC, 2002, Vol. 4, p. 49.

8. "Decree on Priestly Formation," *Documents of Vatican II*, Chapter II, No. 2.

9. Peck, M. Scott, *The Road Less Traveled*, Simon & Schuster, Inc., New York, NY, 1978, pp. 45-46.

10. Ibid., pp. 276-277.

11. *Directory for the Life and Ministry of Priests*, No. 27.

12. Drummond, Thomas B., "Sexual Misbehavior and the Infused Competency Myth," *The New Life Institute for Human Development Newsletter*, The New Life Institute, Middleburg, VA, Winter 2003, Vol. 11, No. 1.

13. Hoge, Dean R., *The First Five Years of the Priesthood*, The Liturgical Press, Collegeville, MN, 2002, p. 101.

14. *The Basic Plan for the Ongoing Formation of Priests*, pp. 95-98.

15. *The Priest and the Third Christian Millennium*, United States Catholic Conference, Washington, DC, 1999, Chapter 4, no. 3.

16. *Origins*, United States Conference of Catholic Bishops, Washington, DC, Vol. 18, no. 31, Jan. 12, 1989.

17. Pope John Paul II, *I Will Give You Shepherds*, St. Paul Books & Media, Boston, MA, 1992, no. 76.

18. Howe, Neil, and William Strauss, *Millennials Rising: The Next Great Generation*, Vintage Books, New York, NY, 2000, pp. 3-29.

CHAPTER 1

A Vision of Unity

––––––– –––––––

THE TWO ARMS OF THE BISHOP: PRESBYTERATE AND DIACONATE

Rev. J. Ronald Knott

As long as Moses kept his hands raised up, Israel had the better of the fight. Moses' hands, however, grew tired. Meanwhile Aaron and Hur supported his hands, one on one side and one on the other, so that his hands remained steady till sunset.

Exodus 17:12

I cannot read the story of Aaron and Hur holding up the arms of Moses without thinking about one of the best descriptions of the diaconate and its relationship to the presbyterate that I have ever read. It is in Walter Cardinal Kasper's book *Leadership in the Church: How Traditional Roles Can Serve the Christian Community Today.* Here is an overview of some of his insights.

One of the great things to come out of Vatican Council II was the restoration of the diaconate. Various motives were proposed for this restoration, including a vision of relieving the pressure of a future priest shortage. The Council, however, rejected this idea because the diaconate is an autonomous grade of the sacrament of orders, not a substitute in places where priests are lacking, nor is it one particular form of lay ministry.

In choosing to go back past medieval developments to early church ordination liturgies and patristic theology, the Council Fathers saw the diaconate as vitally necessary to the life of the church and, with the presbyterate, one ordained ministry, of which the episcopacy is the fullness. The diaconate and the presbyterate, they said, have different tasks and denote two different structures, but they collaborate with one another because both participate in the bishop's ministry and both are immediately subordinate to the bishop.

The Council saw the diaconate and the presbyterate as graded participation in the bishop's ministry. The diaconate is not subordi-

3

nate to the presbyterate. The presbyterate and the diaconate are subordinate to the bishop directly — they are his two arms, so to speak. The deacon is not an "almost priest," nor is he one who fills in the gap where no priests are available.

The main role of the deacon, as the bishop's representative, is to lead, inspire and motivate the whole church to service in collaboration with priests. Deacons do not do service *for* the church, but they make sure the church is doing service. This necessary leadership role does not dispense the laity, the bishop or the priest from their own service tasks. Deacons are charged with promoting the *diakonia* of the whole church — with inspiring, motivating and training others for diaconal service, not just to do service *for* the church.

At liturgy, it is the deacon's responsibility to bring the needs of the community, especially the poor, to the table. It is the deacon who trains and guides volunteers as well as lay ministers. The deacon is the contact person to governmental services. No matter what he is doing, the deacon's role is to make sure the church is serving, not to be an "almost priest" or, as I have experienced on occasion, to be merely a cultic leader who likes to be around the altar wearing liturgical robes and displaying pectoral crosses bigger than the bishop's himself, but who couldn't care less about servant leadership.

Neither priests nor deacons carry out their own ministries. Both help the bishop to carry out his ministry. These gradations of participation in the bishop's ministry denote two separate arms, both having different tasks that must collaborate with one another in unity. That unity is symbolized when the bishop has traditionally worn a chasuable, dalmatic and tunic all at once. In the ministry of the bishop, the presbyterate is one arm of the bishop and the diaconate the other. In a real sense, the diaconate and the presbyterate make the same bishop present in the communities entrusted to them, each in their own way.

Reprinted with permission. This article first appeared in Deacon Digest, Vol. 28, No. 3 (May 2011).

The Spiritual Renewal of the American Priesthood: The Relationship of Bishop and Priest in Ministry

Most Rev. Matthew H. Clark

A. The Framework of a Relationship between Bishop and Priest

The relationship between priest and bishop is crucial to the task of carrying out the mission of the church in our time. On it rises and falls our success in preaching the Gospel and sustaining communities of faith and love.

But there is no one pre-established pattern or framework for that relationship.

Granted, it is good to have a framework that informs and guides the lived relationship between bishop and priests. Such a framework helps us to start from commonly held premises and enhances our capacity to build on solid beginnings. Such an asset also allows for the kind of review and assessment that keeps such relationships alive and growing. Nevertheless, it would be naïve to think that there is but one right way to structure that relationship. Circumstances differ from place to place. Boston is not Rochester is not Wichita is not Chicago. Each has its own history, priorities, resources, problems, possibilities and dreams. We know, too, that no two bishops, no two presbyterates are just the same.

1. Exploring the Lived Reality

If the theory or framework of our relationships is important, no less important are the ways in which we live them out. We do that in a church that is dynamic, on the move, and in a community and a world that are quite complex and challenging; and we do it in a spirit of faith. Sometimes that is a rewarding and life-giving experience for us. We sense that things are moving in a good direction, that our hard work is paying off, that the struggle is very much worthwhile. At other moments, the opposite seems true. We ask or are asked, "Why are we going backwards?"

These issues can be upsetting, even discouraging at times. We like progress to be linear and incremental. We do not like to go backward or to suffer reverses. But the truth is that this kind of experience is part of the fabric of the church's life. It is, therefore, a regular part of the life of the priest and bishop. How we deal with this kind of experience together is, to me, the best test and expression of the relationship we enjoy with one another. In such times, we must go beyond the surface of things and probe the deeper questions: Where is the Spirit leading in all of this? What is the most constructive and honest way to deal with the questions that are before us? How do I/we in constructive fashion negotiate the tensions that exist at this stage of the church's journey?

2. QUESTIONS REMAIN

I confess that I have more questions to offer than I have answers. But let me name a few issues and questions that I think will be best answered if the relationships among us are characterized by honesty, trust and mutual respect:

A. SPEAKING WITH HONESTY AND COURAGE

"Bishops, we need your leadership and support."

The speaker, the chairman of the presbyteral council of one of the eight dioceses of our New York Province, was addressing the bishops of our province on behalf of the members of the priests' councils of New York (PCNY). He was giving voice to the concern of the PCNY that we bishops are not giving them proper leadership and backing as they deal with some of the sensitive issues we are facing today. He was referring to such things as some provisions of the General Instruction to the Sacramentary, of *Dominus Jesus,* of the recent interdicasterial paper on the distinctions between ordained and lay ministry, of documents relating to gay and lesbian issues. He referred not only to the content of these documents but to concerns about how things are being decided in our church today. Their spokesperson indicated that the priests of our province are concerned that the normal processes by which significant pastoral decisions should be made are being short-circuited or overruled by Roman dicasteries.

As best I could understand him, he was saying that it is very difficult for priests to deal with tensions that exist when faithful, smart, committed catholic people are left confused, angry or unsettled by the decisions and processes mentioned above. He was making a request on behalf of the priests to the bishops of the province to be more visible and vocal than we currently are in support of their efforts to deal with these tough questions in local communities.

I admired what the priest said. In my opinion, we bishops do not spend enough time in our provincial meeting dealing with such issues as these. A part of that comes from the fact that we bishops bring a variety of pastoral approaches to any given issue. Sometimes I think that we are reluctant to explore these differences for fear that such discussions will be divisive, indicate disloyalty to the Holy See or will impinge on the legitimate prerogatives of the individual diocesan bishop.

Whatever the reason, I think that the health of our presbyterates, our provinces, our church is enhanced when all of us can speak frankly about matters of importance to us. That does not mean that all is up for grabs or that there is no end to discussion. It simply means that our mutual trust and common faith will sustain honest discussion and help us to move ahead in unity and peace.

B. SEEKING THE COMMON GOOD

"I wish that our Stewardship Council could have heard that discussion."

I quote myself here. The reference is to the quality of so many discussions in our presbyteral council that I wish our diocesan Stewardship Council could have heard. They are rooted in faith, marked by a love for the church, and manifest considerable pastoral wisdom born of long experience. I might also have started this reflection by substituting Presbyteral Council for Stewardship Council. That latter body — so gifted, faithful and accomplished — renders incredible service to our local church in areas I am sure I need not spell out for you.

My point is that one of the challenges of bishops and priests today is to be lead agents in the wedding of the wisdom and expertise of presbyteral councils with the similar gifts of their counterparts of our Stewardship Councils or their equivalents in your respective dioceses. Last year at Techny, the several bishops who gathered were much in agreement that both bodies are much needed for the health and good order of the local churches. My recollection is that all of us were searching for ways in which the two bodies could work in mutual understanding and harmony for the good of the local church. The challenge, I believe, is born not from a thirst for power by either group. Rather, it stems from the fact that the two cultures — the civic or business culture and our church culture — are quite different. They ask us, "Why do you waste so much time consulting everyone? Can't you make a decision?" We ask them, "How do you survive in business with 'fiats' like that?"

I exaggerate, of course, but I do so to illustrate the point that this challenge also holds great opportunity for us. All good gifts are for the common good — the pastoral gifts, the business gifts, the educational and the cultural gifts. They are all meant to build up the body of Christ and to advance the reign of God. I believe that we bishops and priests, working together, have a tremendous contribution to make in this regard. We will be the more credible to our lay counterparts to the degree that they see in our relationships attractive levels of trust, maturity and mutual respect. What I say here about such commonalties I expand to relationships with all leaders in all of our communities. We are not here to compete but to complement, not to be served but to serve.

c. **Facing the Common Challenge**

"Please don't ask me to be a circuit rider. I need to live in a stable community if I am to be a productive minister of the Gospel. I just can't be a sacramental machine that pops in on Sunday morning."

Once again, I exaggerate a bit to make a point. Or do I? Surely, we have all heard such comments and have our own reactions to them. And I would guess that we have all heard from other priests who serve multiple communities and who do so with a great deal of satisfaction and enjoyment. We are all different, so it is not surprising that the same experience elicits different reactions in different priests.

Whatever those reactions may be, most of us are coping in some fashion with the fact that we ordained priests are diminishing in number and, at the same time, are growing older. The ways in which we cope vary from person to person and from place to place, but one of the common notes is our concern for the health and well being of our brother priests. One of my concerns, for example, is that some priests respond to the situation by stretching themselves beyond reasonable limits. Another is the threat to the integrity of local communities because we will not be able at this rate of decline to sustain the Sunday Eucharistic liturgy in all of our parishes.

I do not have magic answers to those challenges. I do believe we need to pray and work for vocations to the priesthood. (I see most priests doing this especially in their generous way of service.) We need to encourage and support well-trained deacons and lay ministers for the service of the people. It is important that we think critically about what is at the heart of priestly ministry so that we use our talent and energy in the best way possible. We must, wherever it is needed, encourage our faithful sisters and brothers to alter formerly legitimate but now unreasonable expectations they have of their priests. It is my hope as well that we will come to the day when the church will revisit the discipline of celibacy as it now exists in the Latin Rite. Such a reflection would yield no magic answers to difficult problems. But because the question is so much alive in the minds of so many people of faith, lay and ordained, I do believe it would do much good if the church were to give that revered discipline a thorough review.

3. Some Conclusions

Why did I go into all of this? I did so for two basic reasons. The first is my conviction that we work together best and grow together when, respecting the church's deepest tradition, we can share with our brother bishops, priests, co-ministers and the whole church the honest questions that are on our minds. The second reason is my belief that we ordained priests will best serve the church in these demanding times if we (A) work together in service of God's holy people and (B) acknowledge in the doing that we are different one from the other, that these differences should not divide us one from the other, but enhance our common work.

B. A Theological Reflection on Relationship

To break open the relationship between priest and bishop so that it can be better understood, I think it beneficial for us first to understand the essentially relational character of these two distinct ecclesial ministries.

1. The Bishop as a Member of the Episcopal College

When a man is ordained a bishop, his ordination brings with it membership in the college of bishops, which, together with and under the pope, exercises supreme authority in the universal church. This is the highest calling of his episcopal office. It is because he is first a member of this college, because he is first in relationship with his brother bishops and the pope, that he becomes an overseer of a particular local church and not the other way around.

The apostolic college, called into existence by the Lord Jesus as he himself summoned his apostles, was not made up of local bishops. Hence, according to theologian Karl Rahner, the college of bishops ...

> "is not simply the union of local bishops as such, but a collegial governing board in the church which cannot as such derive its authority from the locally limited authority of its members as local bishops." (TI: 6, 323)

The authority of the college derives from the authority of the apostles themselves whom Jesus sent in His name. Likewise the authority of the individual bishop, as a successor of the apostles, derives from Christ himself. In our theology, bishops are collegial brothers of the Bishop of Rome and are not his delegates or his branch managers. The Second Vatican Council's "Dogmatic Constitution on the Church" *(Lumen Gentium)* expressed it this way:

> "Bishops govern the particular churches entrusted to them as the vicars and ambassadors of Christ... Their power, which they personally exercise in Christ's name, is proper, ordinary and immediate... Nor are they to be regarded as vicars of the Roman Pontiff, for they exercise an authority which is proper to them..." (#27)

As members of the college, bishops individually and collectively bear a responsibility for all the churches. In the Roman Pontificate the bishop-elect is admonished:

> "Never forget that in the Catholic Church, made one by the bond of Christian love, you are incorporated into the college of bishops. You should therefore have a constant concern for all the churches and gladly come to the aid and support of churches in need. Attend to the whole flock in which the Holy Spirit appoints you an overseer of the church of God."

Material relief of the churches in need has been a hallmark of Christianity from the time in the ancient church when St. Paul took up collections to help the "poor among the saints at Jerusalem." (Rom 15:26)

But an even more important way in which a bishop carries out his concern for the whole church is by making his own diocese a living, vibrant contributing member of the universal church, sharing its local spiritual riches with the whole. For example, the churches of Latin America, existing in a different socio-economic situation from the American or European churches, have helped the whole church to understand the Gospel as a call to liberate people from oppression. The churches of Asia, in dialogue with indigenous religions, have been able to bring a new dimension to our understanding of the Gospel and of God's salvific will to save all peoples in Jesus Christ. The unique contribution of all the particular churches helps us to see the rich diversity that can exist within the unity of the universal church.

2. The Priest as a Member of a Presbyteral College

This long introduction about the episcopacy, detailing its relationship first to the college of bishops with the pope as its head and then to a local church, was necessary to set the stage for a discussion of the presbyterate, which has its own bipolar relationship to a college and to a particular community.

Just as the bishop by his episcopal ordination enters into the college of bishops, so the priest by the laying on of hands enters into a college, the presbyterium of the local church.

Judging by the witness of the New Testament and other early Christian documents, the ancient church never thought in terms of a solitary priest but only of a presbyterium, united with the local bishop. The presbyterium was not simply a collection of parish priests residing in places where there was no bishop. It was a college that surrounded the bishop, helping him to do the work of the church.

In recovering this understanding, the Second Vatican Council in its document on the "Ministry and Life of Priests" *(Presbyterorum Ordinis)* speaks of the priesthood as "joined to the episcopal order" and therefore sharing "in the authority with which Christ himself constitutes, sanctifies and rules his body." (#2)

According to the Council, then, priests do not take the place of the bishop in a parish. Rather, in the priests, the bishop is present to the whole of the local church, in all its communities, in all of its parishes.

Of course, this is why the church does not ordain a priest for a particular parish. Rather, he is ordained as a member of the presbyterium of a local church. Only secondarily is he assigned to a particular community. Once he is appointed to a parish, it is to be expected that most of his responsibility will be for that parish. Yet he must not forget that two relationships simultaneously claim his attention, namely (1) concern for the whole local church and (2) concern for his parish. Though his parish may demand most of his time, it does not lessen the importance of his prior commitment to the diocesan church.

Just as the bishop of a diocese must share his local church's wealth with the universal church, so too the individual parish, blessed with material goods, must share these gifts of God with the whole.

More importantly, just as the bishop of the local church enriches the universal church by offering to it the experiences of and insights into the Gospel that take place in the local church, so the pastor of a parish can bring to the diocese the treasures of how people are living the mystery of the dying and rising of Jesus in their lives. Urban parishes will be able to contribute spiritual insights different from those of suburban and rural parishes. All can contribute to the building up of the local church.

3. Pastoral Implications of this Relationship

Theologically, the relationship between the pope and bishops is not an exact reproduction of the relationship between a bishop and his priests. Recall that bishops are successors of the apostles and exercise authority in their dioceses as vicars of Christ and not representatives of the pope. Nevertheless, the relationship between bishop and priest is truly collegial. Pastors, while they enjoy ordinary jurisdiction in their parishes, are nevertheless an "extension," as it were, of the bishop and the presbyterium. Through the disbursed presbyterium, the bishop is made present throughout the entire diocese.

Pastors symbolize the presence of the bishop and make his pastoral concern present. For this reason the bishop needs to "dialogue with his priests, individually and collectively, not merely occasionally, but if possible, regularly" (CD 28) in order to know the people and their needs. He needs to be in close touch with his priests, listening to the wisdom and insight they bring from the communities among whom they minister in order to form with them pastoral strategies that will allow the Gospel to break into our world in new and effective ways. Without this relationship, our sacred mission fails.

C. Some Experiences of this Relationship that Shape our Understanding

1. Priests' Associations

Shortly after the Second Vatican Council, priests' associations sprang into existence in response to the Council's suggestion that such groups were "to be highly esteemed and diligently promoted." (PO8) In practice, they quite often became adversarial groups that collectively represented the needs and wants of the diocesan priests to the bishop.

In a sense, especially within the wider context of the culture of the time, they were catalysts of an explosion after years of simmering hostility that had built up between priest and bishop, i.e. between what was often perceived as an unhealthy relationship between child and adult, slave and master, empowered and the powerless or even inmate and warden. Some suggested that such adversarial unions were the byproduct of an ecclesial system that seemed to put more emphasis on outward conformity than on the church's central mission, more emphasis on elaborate regulations on the manner of dress, speech and action than on developing personal spiritual maturity.

Others suggested that the Council itself was to blame. When the bishops of the world gathered in the Second Vatican Council, the newspapers of the world reported that the bishops were actually speaking their minds about triumphalism, clericalism and abuse of power. Quite naturally, when the bishops returned home, the priests wanted their turn to speak their minds but many American bishops were reluctant to listen.

The bishops at council had taught that the laity were to "disclose their needs and desires with that liberty and confidence which befits children of God and brothers of Christ." They taught that the "laity are empowered — indeed sometimes obliged — to manifest their opinion on those things which pertain to the good of the church..." using "institutions established by the Church for that purpose..." (LG 37). But when it came to establishing "a group or senate of priests" so that bishops would have an institution to "listen to their priests' views and even consult them ... about matters that concern the needs of pastoral work and the good of the diocese," the bishops at Vatican II only recommended that such institutions "should" be set up (PO 7). And concerning this, following the Second Vatican Council, many bishops in the United States simply temporized.

Unwittingly, Vatican II had probably contributed to this adversarial relationship between priest and bishop, for the council documents seemed to prize freedom of thought and expression. In its declaration on Religious Liberty *(Dignitatis Humanae)*, for example, the bishops had taught that all men and women, as creatures called to communion with God, have a dignity and freedom that must "be respected as far as possible, and curtailed only when and in so far as necessary." (# 7) Nevertheless, many priests felt trapped, pinned under the bishop's thumb, with their legitimate freedom remaining dramatically and unnecessarily curtailed.

2. Presbyteral Councils

Though much good came out of most priests' councils in the years following Vatican II, there often remained a strained relationship between priest and bishop that manifested itself in the very structure of the council. Usually, the bishop was not technically a member of the body. The priests elected the members and officers and essentially invited the bishop to hear what the priests had to say on various topics. And he would go away and decide what he wanted to do. As a consequence, in some dioceses, the bishop did not frequently attend priests' council meetings, and when he did, not much was accomplished.

3. The 1983 Revision of the Code of Canon Law

With the promulgation of the 1983 Code came a new beginning for the presbyteral council. By then, much of the negative energy of the '60s and '70s had dissipated, and the renewal of this vital consultative body became possible.

According to the code, the bishop was no longer an appendage. He was the one to convoke the council and preside over it because, as Vatican II had taught 18 years before, "all priests, whether diocesan or religious, share and exercise with the bishop the one priesthood of Christ. They are thus constituted providential cooperators of this episcopal order." *(Christus Dominus 28)*

The role of the council also became clarified at this time. According to canon 495, it was to assist the bishop in the governance of the diocese, promoting as much as possible the pastoral good of the people. In its *Constitution on Bishops in the Church (Christus Dominus)*, Vatican II had ideally hoped that disagreements would never get in the way of the mission. It wrote:

> "The relations between the bishop and the diocesan clergy should be based before all else on supernatural charity, so that their unity of purpose will make their pastoral activity more effective." (28)

But this supernatural charity was often wanting, and the mission often suffered as a result. This all began to change once both bishop and priests became battered enough through the day-to-day existence of post-conciliar ministry to begin to stop talking past each other.

4. The Effects of Decline

Priests began to sympathize with their bishops once they began to see what a human toll it was taking on their numbers: some bishops got caught up in sex and finance scandals, others in alcohol and drug addiction, and still others broken by various health concerns — often as the result of stress. Priests began to understand how real were Pope Paul VI's words: "To be a bishop today is a more demanding, difficult and perhaps, humanly speaking, more thankless and dangerous task than ever before." (AAS 58:69)

And the bishops began to realize what an emotional toll the aging and declining number of priests had taken on the morale of their ministers. Many priests had become absolutely terrified about the future. Both bishops and priests have realized as never before that it is only together that the Gospel will be effectively preached to a new generation of Roman Catholics.

D. A Turn to the Ideal

1. The Ideal Basis of Any Relationship

The New Testament offers us many insights into human relationships that, if taken together, suggest a principle that can illuminate for us the ideal relationship between priest and bishop.

For example, at a time when men and women were not equal in society, St. Paul nevertheless told the Corinthian church that the husband is the sanctifier of the wife and the wife is the sanctifier of the husband. (1 Co 7:14)

When masters still owned slaves as property, St. Paul wrote to Philemon that the runaway slave, Onesimus, was sent back "no longer as a slave but more than a slave, as a beloved brother." (Phil 15)

Again, at a time when the household codes proscribed the husband as the head of the wife, the writer of the Letter to the Ephesians could nonetheless teach: "Defer to one another out of reverence for Christ." (Eph 5: 21)

One could conclude, therefore, that the basic principle of Christian relationship is equality, despite one's position or ministry, or social standing.

2. Applying the Ideal to the Bishop's Life

When we turn to Vatican II's "Decree on the Ministry and Life of Priests" *(Prestyterorum Ordinis)*, we read the following:

> "On account of this common sharing in the same priesthood and ministry then, bishops are to regard their priests as brothers and friends and are to take the greatest interest they are capable of in their temporal and spiritual welfare. For on their shoulders particularly falls the burden of sanctifying their priests: therefore they are to exercise the greatest care in the progressive formation of their diocesan body of priests. They should be glad to listen to their priests' views and even consult them and hold conferences with them about matters that concern the needs of the pastoral work and the good of the diocese." (7)

If indeed the Christian ideal is that the priest and bishop are equal in dignity and call, then what is said here of the bishop's task can be likewise said of the priest's task vis-à-vis the bishop.

Bishops get isolated in the local church because of their ministry, authority and responsibility. Some then become uncomfortable among the priests… guarded, distant. But isn't it the presbyterium's responsibility to make a bishop to feel welcome? Isn't it their task to treat him as brother and friend, looking out for his spiritual and temporal welfare? Do the priests as a body understand it as their duty to see to the sanctification of their bishop? To his ongoing formation? To his health and development? Is the presbyterium ready to listen to what he is really saying and to consult with him before a crisis looms? Or is he only the distant father figure, the lonely prophet who must find nourishment and sustenance on his own?

3. Applying the Ideal to the Life of the Presbyterium

Once again we turn to Vatican II's *Decree on the Ministry and Life of Priests*, where we read:

"Priests for their part should keep in mind the fullness of the sacrament of Order which bishops enjoy and should reverence in their persons the authority of Christ, the supreme Pastor. They should therefore be attached to their bishop with sincere charity and obedience. That priestly obedience, inspired through and through by the spirit of cooperation, is based on that sharing of the episcopal ministry which is conferred on priests by the sacrament of Order and the canonical mission." (7)

If indeed the Christian ideal is that the priest and bishop are equal in dignity and call, then what is said here of the priest's task can be likewise said of the bishop's task vis-à-vis the priest.

Priests in many dioceses report feeling that the bishop does not reverence them. Some are simply put off by his office. Others feel in his presence like a minion, a foot soldier, a cipher. These feelings are often compounded by a sense that the priest is neither respected by the bishop on the diocesan level nor by the people he serves on the parish level. Rather, in both spheres, he is more often than not corrected for his faults and reminded of his deficiencies. Few notice nor seem to care about the good that he accomplishes day in and day out.

But if the bishop were to find in him something special, a person with a vocation to be honored, a birthday and anniversary to be celebrated, whose words were worth listening to, whose pain was understood and whose loneliness was shared, then cooperation would become easy, and collaboration would be a joy.

Where we've failed is not in the great and glorious schemes. We've done them pretty well. We've failed in the little things.

It is not a professional workshop we need to make priest and bishop function more effectively. It's to look at their relationship with new eyes and to discover again the Gospel call to exercise authority as service, to become for each other the servant of all.

4. Institutionalizing the Ideal

The history of the church demonstrates the importance of capturing evangelical ideals in institutional form. While we know that institutions have a tendency to solidify and smother an ideal, without institutions to serve an ideal, carry on an ideal, promote and honor an ideal, it can very quickly die.

Consequently, Vatican II did not simply urge a bishop to be "solicitous for the welfare — spiritual, intellectual, and material — of his priests" (CD 16); it recommended concrete courses of action to guarantee that it would happen. It recommended scheduling academic courses, arranging for special conferences and planning extended retreats. In the years since the Council, many bishops have called together all their priests in convocation for fruitful dialogue or established lecture series or created study weeks where priest and bishop can learn together. Moreover, bishops have created institutionalized ways to increase the social interaction between priests and bishop, whether in feting those who celebrate significant anniversaries or in honoring those to be singled out for special recognition.

Even with such institutions, both bishop and priest need to be cautious. Without a genuine mutual respect, love and care for each other, which must undergird all such interactions, these institutions can quickly devolve into a modern form of paternalism. Or worse yet, they can become bureaucratic barriers that serve only to further separate the bishop from his priests.

E. The Presbyterium: No Such Thing as a Relationship in Isolation

1. The Catholic Church is Built on the Principle of Unity

At the very end of the first century, Ignatius of Antioch wrote a letter to the Christians at Smyrna to warn them against the schismatics who were claiming that Jesus never had a human body. Encouraging them thus, he wrote:

> "Shun schisms, as the source of troubles. Let all follow the bishop as Jesus Christ did the Father, and the priests as you would the Apostles. Reverence the deacons as you would the command of

God. Apart from the bishop, let no one perform any of the functions that pertain to the Church ... Wherever the bishop appears, there let the people be; as wherever Jesus Christ is, there is the Catholic Church." (8)

This is the first time that anyone had used the expression "the Catholic Church." Ignatius used it to distinguish the schismatics from that true Church of God that had spread throughout the "catholica." It was a way for Ignatius to contrast the eccentric schismatics from the local church, which gathered loyally around its bishop and universally around Jesus Christ.

Ignatius could countenance neither disunity in the local church nor disunity in the Great church universal. Both, he taught, served the cause of the devil.

2. The Local Presbyterium and the Church Universal

We have seen that the relationship between priest and bishop is both personal and ministerial. It cannot exist in the abstract and is only real insofar as it is expressed in a loving communion that is focused on the mission of preaching the Gospel, gathering into community, worshipping God and serving those in need.

But this mission is not merely a local task. And neither are the relationships by which it is best accomplished. The mission is the mission of Jesus Christ, entrusted not to a single community alone but to an apostolic college, and by extension to the churches under their care.

Please recall how I began this talk — with reference to the relationship that is prior to every other relationship the bishop enters into: his relationship to the episcopal college which, together with and under the pope, exercises supreme authority in the universal church. Though he remains rooted in a local church, which he serves with heart and soul, he must at one and the same time serve the needs of the Great Church as well.

It goes without saying that there can be considerable tension between the bishop's local and universal roles, since what may seem good and life-giving for his local church may prove detrimental in some way to the whole. The bishop should not feel alone and isolated in handling this tension. After all, he is bound by bonds of supernatural charity to the members of his local presbyterium, who must help him make this tension understandable to the local church.

As we have pointed out, priests bring their personal and ministerial hopes and cares, their dreams and their failures to their bishop, sometimes singly but more often in such gatherings as the presbyteral council. There both priest and bishop search for pastoral strategies to answer the needs of the people under their care. It is there also that they look for ways to present the issues that concern the Great Church to the people who live out their faith in the communities they shepherd.

In similar fashion, the bishop represents the hopes and cares, the dreams and failures of his particular church to the Great Church, in a process meant to enrich the life of all. While our theology says that the Great Church, often in the person of the bishop of Rome or the Roman Congregations that serve the church in his name, may limit a bishop's authority in his diocese in a particular way only for the sake of the whole People of God, it is often not experienced that way. Bishops, who by divine right ought to be jointly exercising supreme authority in the church with and under the pope, are not consulted about matters of faith, matters of discipline or even matters of pastoral strategy.

Vatican II reminded the church that it is unity and not uniformity that the Church of Rome seeks. Our theology teaches that the pope "presides over the whole assembly of charity and protects legitimate differences." (LG 13) But the lived reality is too often lately something different. Many bishops — and through and with them priests, pastoral ministers and wonderful faithful people — feel left out, diminished, unheard, put down when the Church of Rome acts in isolation. It is a situation that must be addressed, if not in this pontificate then surely in the next.

3. THE TEST OF RELATIONSHIP: UNITY IN CHARITY

Despite our sense of frustration, there can be no bitterness or anger. As Ignatius of Antioch put it, "Wherever there is division or anger, God has no place." (Phil 8) Rather, we, priests and bishop, must model for the local church a unity in faith and love that embraces the Great Church despite her imperfections, knowing that we have imperfections of our own. We must model a loving relationship that, despite the strain, continues to work at the mission, continues to build up those being saved.

Besides, as local churches we have to beware of perspectivism, a tendency to view things only from our own point of view. It is all too easy to hide behind one's prejudices, to get lost in one's own opinions. While we may not always understand the Great Church's perspective, we know from history that it is often a healthy corrective to our own narrow view.

Having said this, I also know from history that the Great Church has sometimes tried to resolve the tension between particular and universal in a most unsatisfactory way, becoming repressive and reactionary and truly destructive to the life of the local churches. It only regains its vitality when once again it recalls that the key to ecclesiology is relationship.

As local churches, we aid in that rediscovery every time we act among ourselves as we wish the church universal to act, in a relationship of mutual respect and love.

Working together, priest and bishop must create a model for the Great Church in which difficult questions are open for discussion, where people and ministers share their faith and their doubts, where men and women "come to decisions on their own judgment in the light of truth, govern their activities with a sense of responsibility, and strive after what is true and right, willing always to join with others in cooperative effort." (DH 8)

This talk was given on October 24, 2000, at the National Federation of Priests' Councils, Spiritual Renewal Project, Divine Word International, Techny, Illinois. Permission granted by National Federation of Priests' Councils and Bishop Matthew Clark.

THE PRESBYTERIUM OF THE DIOCESE

Rev. Gary Coulter

Addressing the U.S. Bishops of Detroit and Cincinnati on their Ad Limina visit (May 6, 2004), Pope John Paul II said, "Strengthening a spirituality of communion and mission will demand a constant effort to renew the bonds of fraternal unity within the presbyterate." As he elaborates on the Bishop's role:

> Precisely because the members of his presbyterate are his closest cooperators in the ordained ministry, each Bishop should constantly strive to relate to them "as a father and brother who loves them, listens to them, welcomes them, corrects them, supports them, seeks their cooperation and, as much as possible, is concerned for their human, spiritual, ministerial and financial well-being" (*Pastores Gregis*, 47).

All priests are familiar with the presbyteral order, that relationship among all priests from their identity with Christ the High Priest received in Holy Orders. Yet the Holy Father, speaking about the "presbyterate," here seems to refer to something more, a bond and grouping that takes place among the priests and with the bishop in a diocese. This occurs because after ordination, priests receive a specific pastoral mission. They are not simply serving the whole Church, but fully dedicate themselves to a particular Church and the faithful who compose it. This is the basis of the "presbyterium."

The Second Vatican Council reappraised and renewed this concept of the presbyterium: the role priests have in collaborating with each other and with the bishop in the ministry and governance of a particular Church. This concept came from the ecclesiological and theological renewal made by the Council, yet is based upon an already-existing tradition in the writings of the early Church. This article will trace a brief history of the presbyterium in order to see the value of the presbyterium acting with its bishop.

TERMINOLOGY AND TRANSLATION

The Second Vatican Council used the Latin word *presbyterium* with a specific meaning. It refers to the body of priests who exercise pastoral offices in a diocese or other particular Church. There is a special bond and relationship created among those priests who, united to their bishop, form a presbyterium.

The Holy Father used the term in this way in the quotes cited above. Unfortunately, the English word presbyterate has two different meanings: 1. *the ordo presbyterorum*, the priesthood, as the second rank of holy orders; 2. *the presbyterium*, the union of all priests in pastoral ministry with the diocesan bishop. In both cases there is a sacramental bond, but in the second, this bond is specified by a common mission, a commitment to work in a particular diocese.

Since English uses the word presbyterate to translate two concepts, the difference between them is often concealed, as the word presbyterate does not contain the fullness of the term presbyterium. Therefore, *I propose that it should be untranslated in English*, as was done in the translations of the Code of Canon Law. Unfortunately, this was not done in the commonly-used Flannery translation of the documents of Vatican II, nor in the official translation of the Directory on the Ministry and Life of Priests. It is contrary to the intention of the Council to equate the presbyterium of a diocese with the universal priesthood.

Scriptural Foundations

Our Lord Jesus called and appointed men whom he would send to preach the Kingdom of God, to share in his power and sanctify and govern the disciples, and thus spread his Church. To continue this mission the apostles appointed other men as successors to replace them, thus preserving the apostolic ministry and tradition in the Bishops of the Church. Yet Christ himself also chose other disciples and helpers to spread the Gospel (Luke 10:1), and so the apostles chose to appoint helpers in their ministry (Acts 6:2-7). As different ministries developed in the early Church, we see two stable groups as helpers of the episcopate and sharers in its authority: the presbyterate and the diaconate.

There is some obscurity of the exact origins of the presbyterate in the New Testament, although it is clear that the word presbyter (*presbyteros*) means elder. A council of elders (*presbyterion*) was present in many apostolic communities. The presbyters clearly fulfilled an important role in the community as pastors and teachers (1 Pet. 5:1-3). Moreover, the presbyter's ministry is linked to the laying on of hands. "Do not neglect the gift you have, which was given ... when the council of elders laid their hands upon you" (1 Tim. 4:14). From this passage one can deduce that the presbyters play a role in the transmission of the apostolic mission.

It seems, however, that this group did not exercise supreme power, as they would be subject to the Apostles (cf. Acts 15:6; 21:18). The part played by the presbyterium, or body of priests, was a very important one in the earlier days of the Church; nevertheless it did not exclude the existence of a monarchic episcopate, the bishop-overseer (*episcopos*) who presided over the presbyters.

IN THE EARLY FATHERS OF THE CHURCH

Writing at the start of the second century, St. Ignatius of Antioch provides a clear idea of the threefold ministry we know today.

I exhort you to strive to do all things in harmony with God: the bishop is to preside in the place of God, while the presbyters are to function as the council of the Apostles, and the deacons, who are most dear to me, are entrusted with the ministry of Jesus Christ (Magnesians 6:1).

St. Ignatius speaks often of the presbyters, but normally refers to them as a council; in Greek: presbyterion, in Latin: presbyterium. The primary idea of St. Ignatius concerning the presbyterium is that priests remain in close union with one another and have a strong bond with their bishop. Thus his famous analogy: "Your presbytery, which is a credit to its name, is a credit to God; for it harmonizes with the bishop as completely as the strings with a harp" (Ephesians 4:1).

His letters frequently indicate that the presbyterium acted as a collective body: a band, college, council or senate. For Ignatius, this collegiality is always characteristic of the presbyterium. Indeed, whenever the Patristic Fathers of the first three centuries mention presbyters, they always speak of them in the plural and never in the singular: they always constitute a college.

Notice that the relationship Ignatius describes between the bishop and presbyters is not one of equality: the presbyterium is subject to the bishop, who presides over them as Christ over the apostles. On the other hand, as the bishop's senate, the college of presbyters shares with him the responsibility for the well being of the ecclesial community. Saints Clement of Rome and Cyprian of Carthage are just two important examples of the many other Church fathers who describe presbyters as constituting a council and being counselors of the bishop.

From the New Testament and early Christian writings, we see that the ancient Church did not think in terms of solitary priests but of a presbyterium. United with the local bishop, it was a college that surrounded him and helped him to carry out the work of the church.

The Loss of the Concept

So what happened to the presbyterium and this idea of the collaboration of the presbyters? As the Church expanded after the legalization of Christianity, priests were stationed outside the episcopal city in order to administer the sacraments in rural districts. This physical separation from the city where the presbyterium would meet limited the priests' participation in it.

With the spread of the gospel into rural areas, isolated from the episcopal city and the presbyterium, the presbyters' role declined as counselors who assisted the bishop in administration. In its place, other bodies developed, such as the Cathedral Chapter and the Diocesan Synod, which continued some of the presbyterium's advisory and governing functions.

Another historical factor that encouraged individualism was development of the benefice system, by which priests were ordained for a particular benefice, a ministry to a particular church or benefactor who guaranteed his economic sustenance. This contributed to a decline in the common life and collaboration among priests, as they would feel less of a bond to the bishop than to their benefactor.

Some also see individualism coming from the developing theology on the priesthood that would culminate with the council of Trent. Of course, nothing is wrong with emphasizing the character of the priest as representing Christ, with a special dignity and personal power to celebrate the Eucharist. This idea, however, should not lead to a separation of the priest from the community or to an individualism or competitiveness in pastoral work.

With the spread of the Church, there was a general breakdown of the early collegiality and a trend toward an individual, not collegiate, ministry. The conception of presbyteral community, as well as knowledge of the meaning of the word presbyterium itself, was slowly lost in centuries of neglect.

IN THE SECOND VATICAN COUNCIL

Without doubt, one of the most central themes of the Second Vatican Council was the Church as communion. This included a desire to restore the communion and collegiality that existed in the early Church between the bishop and his priests in order to strengthen the bond between them. There was a realization that both bishop and priests need to work together, making a common effort for the salvation of souls in the diocese.

During the drafting of *Lumen Gentium*, the decision was made to revive the term presbyterium, based on St. Ignatius of Antioch's notion of the close union existing among presbyters and their bishop. In speaking on the hierarchical structure of the Church, the Council Fathers stress the bond of unity as "the priests ... constitute, together with their bishop, a unique *presbyterium*" (LG 28).

Presbyterium Ordinis begins with an ontological, sacramental definition of the priesthood. Priests "are signed with a special character and so are configured to Christ the priest in such a way that they are able to act in the person of Christ the head" (PO 2). Yet how this ontological reality is actually, concretely lived is shown by articles 7-9, entitled the "Priests' Relation With Others," which discuss his relation towards the bishop, his fellow priests and the laity he serves. The priesthood is lived out within a local, particular church, which is normally the diocese.

Thus, another theological development of the Council was the deepening of the reality of the particular Church. The diocese is not complete if seen only as the bishop and the people. The presbyterium is a constitutive element of the diocese. "A diocese is a section of the People of God entrusted to a bishop to be guided by him with the assistance of his *presbyterium*" (*Christus Dominus* 11). Presbyters are not simply useful for the bishop, but necessary collaborators for him to carry out his mission (PO 7).

The sacrament of holy orders links bishops and priests together, yet the Council has developed something more. "All priests, who are constituted in order of priesthood by the sacrament of Order, are bound together by an intimate sacramental brotherhood; but in a special way they form one *presbyterium* in the diocese to which they are attached under their own bishop" (PO 8).

In the Council's view, the presbyterium does not exist simply for the practical reason of creating a more effective ministry (which it certainly can); rather, it is an intrinsic part of a priest being in hierarchical communion with his bishop. This is also a reason why the presbyterium can include religious priests, not just diocesan priests, when they, too, serve the care of souls and apostolic activity in the particular church.

We can conclude that a concept of the presbyterium emerges from the Council: the group of priests who, at the disposition of the bishop, with him and under his authority, are fully dedicated to the service of a diocese. *The Lex Ecclesiae Fundamentalis* composed after the Council, although not promulgated, still summarizes the Church definition of the presbyterium in a legal way:

Presbyters (as established by Ordination in the Order of the presbyterate) are all mutually connected by an intimate sacramental fraternity; however, they who are assigned to the service of a certain particular Church under their proper Bishop ... form with the Bishop one presbyterium, whose task it is to be for assistance to the Bishop in shepherding the people in the ways determined by law (Can. 48).

The revival of the idea of the presbyterium, which had been lost to theological thought, is one of the great fruits of the Second Vatican Council. A new awareness of this reality of the presbyterium can help priests to apply and implement the teachings of the Council as well as combat feelings of personal loneliness and isolation. Not only is it a call for fraternal charity and brotherhood among priests, but much more, the presbyterium is a mission guiding priests to collaborate and participate within the diocese for a more fruitful ministry.

Reverend Gary Coulter is a priest of the Diocese of Lincoln, Nebraska, ordained in 1999. After three years as an assistant pastor and high school teacher, he has just completed two years of Canon Law studies in Rome, receiving his JCL from Santa Croce University. He is now parish pastor in Ashland and Greenwood, Nebraska. His website, located at http://geocities.com/frcoulter, has a variety of Catholic resources and links, including more information on the juridical manifestations of the Presbyterium.

© *Ignatius Press, April 2005*
Permission received from HPR

From Neglect to Intention: Taking the "Radical Communitarian Dimension of Ordained Ministry" Seriously

Address given at the USCCB Special Assembly
June 17, 2010
Rev. J. Ronald Knott
Respondent to Archbishop Carlson

I can't begin to tell you how honored I am by this invitation. I was actually shocked when the invitation came from Archbishop Lucas while I was leading the 2009 Salt Lake City presbyteral assembly. I know many of you from many such assemblies and study days.

Let me quickly thank Archbishop Thomas Kelly, my former bishop, for allowing me to get into this work and Archbishop Joseph Kurtz, my present bishop, for allowing me to continue.

My time is short and I have much to say, so let me get right to it. As a response to Archbishop Carlson, I want to do three things: (a) tell you quickly how I got into this work, (b) tell you what I have learned, and finally, (c) issue you an invitation.

How I Got Into This Ministry

2002 was the worst year of my 40-year-old priesthood. I was a vocation director the year the sexual abuse scandal broke across the country. I never felt more powerless and more demoralized than I did back then. For the first time in my life, I seriously wanted to quit.

At my very lowest point, I sat down at my computer one day to delete and destroy the ideas that I had developed over the previous seven years. At the very last second I decided not to delete those ideas, but rather to turn them into a book. I ended up calling the book *Intentional Presbyterates: Claiming Our Common Sense of Purpose as Diocesan Priests*. I sent all of the bishops and Continuing Education Directors a free copy. Since then I have written a *Workbook* to go with it, as well as *From Seminarian to Diocesan Priest: Managing a Successful Transition* and *The Spiritual Leadership of a Parish Priest: On Being Good and Good At It*. All address, one way or another, the need for "intentional presbyterates."

Ten thousand copies of *Intentional Presbyterates* have been read by American priests and studied by seminarians in several US seminaries, as well as by priests and seminarians in India, Zambia, Tanzania, Singapore, Kenya, the Philippines and several others, I am told. I have spoken to nearly 100 presbyterates in this country and abroad about presbyteral unity. I just got back from Tuam in Ireland and Winnipeg in Canada. After this I will go to Cardiff in Wales. This fall and next year I have several more assemblies on my calendar, including ones in the Kingdom of Tonga and its neighboring island nation, the Bahamas, and India. Two years ago I was given the chance to address the Priest Councils of England and Wales in Leeds. Our National Federation of Priest Councils has recognized my work with their Touchstone Award. Five years ago I couldn't have imagined this day. Standing here in front of you today to talk about presbyterates is something I could never have imagined a few years back!

I am honored to add my comments to those of Archbishop Carlson. We know each other a bit. I have even met his dogs. I conducted a presbyteral unity workshop in his old diocese of Sioux Falls right after he left and later in his former diocese of Saginaw with him present. You will see that we agree in many areas, and I am honored to be quoted by him in his presentation.

What I Have Learned

1. US priests, in general, have had no formal education in the theology of presbyterates. As a result of this neglect, many priests have fallen into the habit of a priesthood of "private practice," which flies in the face of the "radical communitarian dimension of ordained ministry" that Pope John Paul II was so adamant

about. Even though Canon 245.2 called for seminarians to be trained to take their places in presbyterates, when I started this it had barely been implemented. As a result of a continuing neglect and lack of a common vision, many of today's young priests are forming "tribes" within their Presbyterates, struggling against other priests over who has the right vision. Some of these "tribes" are actively cultivating members from among seminarians. They groom them in secret, advise them how to "get through" seminary formation programs and which bishops deserve respect and obedience. If problems like these are being caused by neglect, imagine what we could become if we were to become more intentional about strengthening presbyteral unity!

The biggest misconception priests have had of the "intentional presbyterate" idea is that it is about making priests happy. While that may be an important by-product of the process, the main reason for an "intentional presbyterate" is to offer the People of God a more coherent and effective ministry. Archbishop Carlson is right about praying for the unity of priests. *A Priest's Prayer for His Presbyterate* and our *Seminarian's Prayer for his Presbyterate* (available in English and Spanish) that I put together a few years ago is being prayed daily by thousands of priests and seminarians. Based on Church documents, hopefully its sentiments will sink into more and more priests' hearts. Finally, as *Lumen Gentium* taught us, working for presbyteral unity is an essential part of a priest's spiritual life, not something nice to do if we feel like it.

2. US priests, in general, have had no formal education in the diocesan "promise of obedience." As a result, they tend to see obedience mainly in terms of a personal relationship with the bishop that is invoked in cases of emergency, rather than seeing what Pope John Paul II called its "communal relationship with the bishop and the presbyterate as a whole." While seminaries are regularly focusing on celibacy programs, many still neglect to teach "that other promise," the promise of obedience, which, when understood well, is critical in developing a common sense of purpose in our ministry because it has to do with what Pope John Paul II called "non-attachment to one's own preferences and points of view" for the sake of our common ministry.

3. Most bishops, where I have made presentations, have indicated to me that US bishops get no real training in how to lead presbyterates. As a result, bishops may not always know how to direct individual ministry accomplishments toward the ministry goals of the diocese as a whole. Priests are waiting — craving, really — to be led by shepherds with convincing voices. Bishops are the designated leaders of presbyterates, but some may need more help in becoming real leaders of presbyterates.

4. Bishops and presbyterates need to pay better attention to the transition of new priests out of seminary and into ministry, to the transition of priests into first pastorates and to the transition of international priests into new local presbyterates and parishes. Presbyterates need to see themselves as mentoring communities of these newest members and spend more time learning to be such mentoring communities. Presbyterates need to understand how risky it is for both sides for new priests to be made pastors without proper training. Presbyterates need to understand as well that it is risky for both sides to accept international priests without a plan to receive them well.

5. An intense, complete and ongoing study of the teachings in *Pastores Dabo Vobis* and your implementation document, The Basic Plan for the Ongoing Formation of Priests, would do more than anything else to help priests find common theological ground on which to heal ideological differences. As it is, both sides of the divide tend to pick and choose citations from Church documents to bolster their already-arrived-at conclusions.

6. A general acceptance of the theology that the ministry of priests consists in helping the bishop carry out *his* ministry and making *him* present in the places where they serve would do wonders in building a sense of presbyteral unity among priests. This includes more dialogue with priests "on directions to be taken and choices to be made."

7. The best program to promote vocations today, I believe, would be one that is directed at building intentional presbyterates. Young men today will not be attracted to a loose association of "lone rangers," but to the religiously saturated environment of a happy and effective presbyterate with a clear identity and

mission. As Vatican II said so many years ago, "Let priests attract the hearts of young men by their own humble and energetic lives, joyfully pursued, and by brotherly collaboration with their brother priests." If this is true, when we pray for more vocations to the priesthood, we ought to move away from asking God to change his behavior and toward asking God to help us change our behaviors — that we might be more humble and energetic in our individual ministry and see it as our share in a collaborative ministry, especially with our bishop and fellow priests.

8. Seminaries need more ways to introduce reality into their curricula. As seminaries continue to add more and more mandated communal experiences, the numbers of priests living alone continues to rise — some say 58% at present and growing. Seminaries need to prepare young priests to creatively live alone, while working together, by experimenting with small-group living and individual living situations while they are still in the seminary. (To that end I have designed and spearheaded the building of a new "life-skills center' at Saint Meinrad to teach simple healthy cooking, to practice being part of a support group and to prepare for being part of a prayer group. It is to be finished by year's end.) To build more unified presbyterates, seminaries need to teach seminarians to *respect and negotiate* the various cultures of ecclesial life in today's Church rather than conspiring with them in *protecting* them from those cultures. Seminarians should be taught to identify and distinguish their own preferred learning culture from the learning cultures of other priests and be prepared to respectfully engage the needs and assumptions of other priests.

9. What is needed, ultimately, for presbyteral unity is not a new program, but a new mindset. I believe at the root of things is a need for a radical conversion of mind and heart by priests and bishops toward the good of one another. Likewise, we need to replace our downward spiraling talk of diminishment with some upward spiraling talk of abundance. Believing is different from wishing. Believing leads to positive action on our part. Wishing simply waits for others to act on our behalf.

10. The Church cannot afford infighting and demoralization among its priests. We need all hands on deck. We need to start seeing our diversity as a blessing. We must firmly and consistently reject the Rush Limbaugh approach to presbyterates, where we feel free to demonize and attribute the worst possible motives to those with whom we disagree. If every snowflake in an avalanche pleads "not guilty," we must individually reverse the process and begin to practice the spiritual discipline of blessing each other by intentionally looking for goodness to affirm in each other.

An Invitation

In 2005 the Lilly Endowment of Indianapolis gave Saint Meinrad close to $2 million to start its *Institute for Priests and Presbyterates* so that we could implement the USCCB's *Basic Plan for the Ongoing Formation of Priests* in a very serious way. We do ongoing formation, especially for priests in their first five years, as well as ongoing formation of presbyterates in their unity. We are now gearing up to add programs for priests in all ages and stages, as you suggested. None of us, however, including the Lilly Endowment, knew how hungry priests were for presbyteral unity. We were funded to pilot six presbyteral assemblies of our own and underwrite three of NOCERCC's *Cultivating Unity* program. After having done close to 100 personally, I am training two more priests to help me. "The harvest is great but the laborers are few."

Part of the grant calls for a group of bishops to come together for a dialogue and a brainstorming session on how bishops can lead their priests to deeper unity. We have the money to pay for airfare, lodging and a nice stipend for about 10 bishops to come to Saint Meinrad this fall for a couple of days to share ideas on how to bring presbyterates to a deeper sense of unity. If you would like to be part of that gathering, please contact me and we will begin the process of finding a mutually acceptable time.*

Thank you for this honor. The last few years have been a truly wonderful spiritual adventure — a gift that just "keeps on giving" — an adventure that I could not have imagined back in 2003. Thank you.

*Several bishops expressed interest, and some could not work the date chosen into their schedules, but the following bishops were able to attend a day-long dialogue at Saint Meinrad on September 3, 2010. In attendance were:

Bishop Daniel Conlon (Steubenville)
Bishop Michael Hoeppner (Crookston)
Bishop William Medley (Owensboro)
Auxiliary Bishop Lee Piché (St. Paul-Minneapolis)
Auxiliary Bishop Mark Seitz (Dallas)
Bishop Richard Stika (Knoxville)
Bishop Anthony Taylor (Little Rock)
Very Rev. Denis Robinson, OSB, President-Rector, Saint Meinrad Seminary and School of Theology
Rev. J. Ronald Knott, Director, Institute for Priests and Presbyterates

Working Toward Intentional Presbyterates: What Can Priests, Seminaries, Presbyterates and Bishops Do?

Rev. J. Ronald Knott

> *The corporate sense of priestly identity and mission, although not fully developed even in official documents, is clearly emerging as an important direction for the future.*[1]
> The Basic Plan for the Ongoing Formation of Priests

Once we understand the importance of the ongoing formation of presbyterates, the teachings that highlight their essential nature and the divisions that militate against them, the next step is to identify practical strategies to support and nurture presbyteral unity. It is one thing to diagnose a problem, but it is another thing to know what to do to fix it.

Coherent and unified presbyterates will not happen by accident, but by intention. The word "intention" comes from the Latin word *intendere*, meaning "to stretch toward, to aim at." Intention is an act of the will by which that faculty efficaciously desires to reach an end by employing the means. It is a concentration of will to the point of resolve. We have to really want it before we can have it.

Like the original twelve apostles, Christ calls his priests to resist those things that threaten the unity of the group – especially working alone, working too much and working against each other.[2]

What Can Individual Priests Do?

Intentional presbyterates, for the good of individual priests and for the sake of their common mission, are not just a matter of providing the right programs to priests. There are no magic programs.

Only a group change of heart, one heart at a time, will lead to a true renewal of our presbyterates. The power of an "intentional presbyterate" cannot be created and unleashed by priests who have no personal passion for it, nor by priests with the inability to visualize it, nor by priests who simply wish it would happen, but rather by priests who have a burning desire to see it happen, a bishop and leader-priests who have the ability to marshal the troops in unleashing the power of the team and the power to direct individual accomplishments toward a common goal, excellent priestly ministry to the people of God. A changed heart may be the only thing that could lead to new and creative behaviors by individual priests toward their brother priests.

Individual conversion is critical, because factions and diatribes emerge from within the hearts of individual priests. If priests have any hope of having a shared sense of direction and purpose, they must accurately identify and honestly confront the personal attitudes that impede and imperil presbyteral unity: their competition, their clashing ecclesiologies, their clerical envy, their lack of respect for the various backgrounds, languages, cultures and places of origin in their presbyterates that all lead to a priesthood of "private practice." Each and every individual priest must name and confront counter-unity forces within his own heart. Every member of the presbyterate has to change, and the most needed change is a personal conversion toward the good of the group.

A healthy and unified presbyterate cannot happen when everyone in it is doing his own thing. Priests in a presbyterate are like an orchestra rather than a loose association of soloists. Saint Ignatius of Antioch, who spoke often of the presbyterate, said, "Your presbytery, which is a credit to its name, is a credit to God; for it harmonizes with the bishop as completely as the strings with a harp."[3] Without leaders to inspire priests and lead them with a common vision, the visions of little cliques will continue to battle each other over who has the "true" vision. A real leader inspires a shared vision and calls individual priests to greatness in translating that vision into reality.

Priests must begin by focusing not on the forms of religion, but on its essence. As William Penn put it, we need to live like Christ, not argue about Christ. We will never agree on methods of delivering the Gospel, but we can and we must agree on the message of the Gospel.

Priests must do something like the writer of Matthew's Gospel did when he wrote. Like the "householder who took things new and old from his storeroom," the writer of Matthew took the best of the old and the best of the new and put them together in a new paradigm for those who missed their old religious ways but wanted to embrace the life, death and resurrection of Jesus.

Priests might do something similar to what we did at the Cathedral of the Assumption in Louisville, Kentucky, when I was pastor there. The leaders there had the job of renovating a renovation, undoing the extreme violence of an earlier radical renovation. An overly ornate, dark and cluttered old landmark had been totally stripped, painted white and carpeted. Its art treasures had been given away, destroyed or relegated to a museum. Those in charge of leading the project were pulled by both extremes, those who wanted to put it back the way it was in bygone days and those who wanted further modernization. Instead of giving in to either extreme, they settled on a plan to bring back the best of the old and put it with the best of the new in such a way that it would take us into the future. It was not a compromise, where both sides lose something. It was a marriage, where both sides won something. They easily raised the money. There were no demonstrations. Everybody was pleased that they could find a home there.

Priests must clean up their own individual acts, as well. Acting *in persona Christi* can be a heavy burden. The words and deeds of priests have the power to do good or do damage to a degree that other people do not experience. As Bishop Richard Sklba put it, people can be deeply hurt for life by a casual flippant remark or inspired forever by a simple genuine gesture of compassion and kindness. Priests do not need to be reminded how the bad behaviors of a few priests have impacted their lives and the life of the church. Priests must become who we say we are. Transparency is required. Priests are entitled to private lives, but not secret lives. A private life energizes. A secret life takes too much energy to hide and protect. A secret life distracts. A secret life quickly erodes a priest's spiritually and drains him of energy and focus.

Priests must stop the "downward spiraling talk." Downward spiraling talk creates an attitude of hopelessness and an atmosphere that leads them to believe that things are going from bad to worse and nothing can be done about it. Hopeless talk produces hopeless situations. On the other hand, positive, upward spiraling talk can create a different reality. The more attention you shine on hopelessness, the more evidence of it will grow. Shine attention on opportunities and possibilities, and they, too, will multiply lavishly.[4] The biggest shortage in the Catholic church is not money or priests or opportunities, but imagination.

When leaders fail to inspire and lead, priests must claim their personal power, instead of being, to paraphrase George Bernard Shaw, "feverish, selfish little clods of ailments and grievances complaining that the church will not devote itself to making them happy." As Pope John Paul II and the American bishops put it, "All formation, including priestly formation, is ultimately self-formation." When no one comes to their rescue, priests must develop the skills of self-rescue, especially when it comes to feelings of loneliness and feelings of being unappreciated. No presbyterate is strong when the members of it are weak.

Diocesan priests make two solemn promises: celibacy and obedience. (It is good to remember that vowed religious priests working under a diocesan bishop are full members of that presbyterate as long as they are working in that diocese.) Rather than negatives, the promises of celibacy and obedience are meant to free us up for ministry. Priests get extensive formation in celibacy, but not in obedience. Obedience is the neglected stepchild of the priestly promises. Once made, it is often forgotten. Of the two promises, the only one ever heard much about is celibacy, but "that other promise" may be even more important for unified ministry to the people of God.

The promise of obedience has implications beyond the relationship of each individual priest to his bishop. Priests often make this promise without a lot of insight into what it means. While today's seminaries are almost obsessive about celibacy training, this promise is barely mentioned in comparison. Once made, this promise is seldom mentioned again, except in cases of intransigency. As a result, many priests understand it only in a simplistic "yes, boss" kind of way. The promise of obedience includes a promise to his fellow presbyteral members. *Pastores Dabo Vobis* says our promise of obedience is "not the obedience of individual priests relating to authority, but rather an obedience which is deeply part of the unity of the presbyterate." "Priestly obedience should be one of solidarity, based on belonging to a single presbyterate" (III, 28). Shoot me as a heretic, if you must, but because this promise is really a promise to be a "team player" with the bishop and the other members of his presbyterate for the sake of the common purpose they share, this promise, I believe, may be more important to the unity of their mission than celibacy. Being more conscious of, and informed about, their promise of obedience, priests are more likely to remember that they do not carry out their own ministry, but are fellow workers in helping the bishop carry out a common ministry. An expansive understanding of the promise of obedience is the only thing diocesan priests have in their arsenal that speaks directly to their unity as a group, because in it they promise each other to be "team players" with the bishop and with each other. This richer understanding of the promise of obedience will be essential in helping priests toward the renewal of their presbyterates.

What Can Seminaries Do?

Where do we begin to build intentional presbyterates, once individual members are converted to the challenge? We begin building our presbyteral unity in the seminary – by teaching the basic principles of presbyteral theology and by having the presbyterate treat them like "novices," mentoring them into the group throughout their seminary experience. Canon 245.2 says that seminary students are to be formed in such as way that they are prepared for fraternal union with the diocesan presbyterate, whose partners they will be in the service of the church. Even though Canon 245.2 was promulgated in 1983, it is just beginning to be implemented in seminaries like Saint Meinrad School of Theology. Many priests today will tell you that they never had one hour of formation on how to be successful, contributing members of their presbyterates, nor have presbyterates had a coherent way of mentoring new members into the presbyterate once they come out of the seminary. Most of the time it is a haphazard, learn-as-you-go process. This neglect, as I said earlier, is one major reason why so many priests see their ministry from a personal, rather than from a collegial, perspective. A renewal of presbyterates will require basic education on the theology of a presbyterate, starting during the initial formation of the seminary and continuing with ongoing remedial formation for priests already ordained.

Seminaries need to revitalize their pastoral formation programs to be sure that the initial formation of the seminary and the ongoing formation after the seminary flow one into the other in an unbroken and coherent way, as called for by *Pastores Dabo Vobis*.[5] This will require a cooperative effort between seminaries and the ongoing formation directors of the dioceses they serve. This may require the part-time use of more parish priests in the pastoral formation programs of the seminaries and the part-time use of seminary personnel in the ongoing formation programs of dioceses.

Pope John Paul II suggested in *Pastores Dabo Vobis* that it might be a good idea for neighboring dioceses to cooperate in offering ongoing formation programs, especially smaller dioceses.[6] Saint Meinrad School of Theology's Institute for Priests and Presbyterates is presently piloting such a cooperative effort in its attempts to offer inter-diocesan support to priests in their first five years, as well as to whole presbyterates. The regular presence of new priests and young pastors on campus is having a dramatic impact on getting the point across that ongoing formation after ordination is no longer an option. Besides the advantage of having the interaction between priests and priests-to-be, seminaries themselves may be the best places for these serious, ongoing formation programs given the availability of their libraries, food services, chapels, recreation facilities, theology professors, confessors, health facilities, counselors and overnight lodging.

Many dioceses have one or two ordinations a year, making the collapse of the seminary support system somewhat traumatic for many of these new priests. Saint Meinrad School of Theology is piloting an interactive website as a way for young priests to stay in touch with each other, share their wisdom and experience, as well as a way to offer one other solutions to problems they experience – all across diocesan lines. It is a place for sharing such things as homilies, reading suggestions, sacramental policies and even travel ideas. It offers an inter-diocesan support system – a broader support system than that which many individual dioceses can offer them. A new day requires a new way.

Many seminarians today are reacting to what they perceive to be a generation of priests before them who promoted "relativism." The generations before them, in return, tend to see young priests today as brash champions of simplistic "truth." These perceptions of each other are contributing seriously to the ideological battles in presbyterates. With their philosophy and theology departments, seminaries are uniquely placed to be able to teach the weaknesses of each perspective, to offer a richer understanding of "truth" as well as how to work creatively with various points of view. As Father David Couturier, in an article already cited, wrote: "Priests and seminarians need to be able to identify their own learning culture and respectfully engage the needs and assumptions of others. This will require skills, language and methods needed to manage the increasing structural and organizational dynamics of Catholic life." The present name-calling helps no one. Seeking to understand, rather than to be understood, is the key.

WHAT CAN PRESBYTERATES DO?

Paying attention to the transition of young priests out of the seminary and into ministry is vitally important. Everyone is aware of the shortage of new priests, but what often goes unnoticed is the fact that we are also losing 10% to 15% of our new priests in their first five years. One new priest, ordained in 2000, told me recently that 13 out of 19 of his ordination classmates have already left the priesthood.

The transition out of seminary into a presbyterate is a lot like being shoved off a cliff to see if one can fly. One bishop compares newly ordained priests to patients emerging from a long-term intensive care unit. Just as patients are plugged into five or six "IVs," so the seminarian is attached to an elaborate support system. Overnight, upon ordination, that support system is removed. Seminaries may not be doing an adequate job of preparing new priests to take their places in diocesan presbyterates, but presbyterates may be doing a worse job of receiving and mentoring their newest members. Every priest, not just the bishop and vocation director, should see himself as sharing in the work of mentoring new priests into presbyterates. Bishops and priests must stop the practice of introducing new priests to the presbyterate on their ordination days. New priests need to be treated like "novices," even while in the seminary, and be mentored by the group from the very beginning of their acceptance as seminarians.

One way to do that is to make sure seminarians are invited to as many presbyteral gatherings as possible, from the beginning of their theological training. Seminarians should not only be invited to attend, but to participate. They need to hear from their fellow priests, yes – but their fellow priests also need to hear from them. They will need not only individual mentoring, but also mentoring by the group.

The fact that more than twenty-eight percent of all American priests now are foreign-born makes having a plan for mentoring new members into the presbyterate even more critical. The Catholic church in the United States has always had international priests to serve its parishes, and during most of its history has depended on them. In 1791, at the first church synod held in Baltimore, eight percent of the clergy present were foreign-born. At the second plenary council in Baltimore in 1866, thirty of the forty-seven bishops were foreign born. It was not until the 1940s and 1950s that the chronic American priest shortage ceased. This period, contrary to what many Catholics think, was an exception to the rule. The longer term American picture is one of a shortage of American seminarians and an endless effort to recruit priests from overseas.[7]

Failure to mentor seminarians into the presbyterate causes problems for the presbyterate, but failure to mentor foreign-born priests into the presbyterate is a set-up for disaster. Foreign-born priests are not the problem. We need them. The problem is there are so few good programs to assimilate them into the American church and its presbyterates. Orientation to American life and culture, language proficiency, personal support systems, the education of the entire presbyterate on their country of origin, and regular visits home are only a few of their needs. Failure to have a well-organized program in place when these priests are accepted is bad for the priests and the people they serve. It is not fair, it is counter-productive and it borders on abuse.

A healthy and effective presbyterate is probably the one best way to replicate itself. All the studies tell us that healthy contact with priests is the reason most young adults make the move toward answering their call to ordained priesthood. One happy and effective priest can do more to promote vocations to diocesan priesthood than a hundred eye-catching billboards. A team of happy and effective priests can do more to promote vocations to diocesan priesthood than a million dollars' worth of clever TV spots. The Second Vatican Council got it right when it said, "Let him attract the hearts of young people to the priesthood by his own humble and energetic life, joyfully pursued, and by love for his fellow priests and brotherly collaboration with them."[8]

Like it or not, this generation of young people will not be attracted to a loose association of "Lone Ranger" priests doing their own thing. What will be attractive to them will be a religiously saturated environment that will bestow a special sense of sacred identity that a unified presbyterate will offer. If this sense of identity and a clearly defined common mission is not offered to them, they will seek that identity and sense of mission in small ideological groups. Young priests have a strong need for belonging. Maybe this is one reason why tension caused by ideological struggles was rated "strong" among 40% of young diocesan priests, while among only 20% of religious priests, according to a recent Dean Hoge study, *Experiences of Priests Ordained Five to Nine Years*.[9]

WHAT CAN BISHOPS DO?

The responsibility for building presbyteral unity falls squarely on the shoulders of the bishop. As noted earlier, the bishops themselves are aware of the fact that this valuable work can often slip to the lower end of a list of priorities, causing a number of attendant problems.

Obvious to anybody who has been around hundreds of priests in this country on a regular basis is the need for new bishops to receive some formation on how to lead a presbyterate so as to be able to unleash the power of the team. Practical suggestions for the ongoing formation of his presbyterate should be a major part of his orientation as a bishop. Priests need effective leadership. There is a growing appetite for presbyteral unity among priests. In many ways, this appetite is waiting to be satisfied by skillful shepherds.

If bishops are not clear about what they expect from their priests, they should not be surprised by the muddled, and sometimes sloppy, responses they get from their priests. A bishop would be wise, in consultation with his presbyterate, to develop a carefully developed list of "talking points" to be used at least when seminarians go off to the seminary, when seminarians are about to be ordained and before priests receive their assignments, especially pastorates. It is especially at these times that formation could be done to insure a common vision.

In many dioceses, there are several offices that deal with the ministry and lives of priests, but more often than not, there is no formal and regular collaboration among the vocation director, the priest council president, the priest personnel director, the ongoing formation director, the priest health panel and the vicar for retired priests. This compartmentalization of priesthood tends to divide priests from each other, priests from the priests-to-be and active priests from retired priests. When this happens, priests conclude that it is the job of the vocation director to promote vocations, the job of the Vicar for Clergy to deal with retired priests and the job of the health panel to death with sick priests. Would it not benefit presbyterates for bishops to gather all these leaders into a "priestly life and ministry cluster" to look at priests holistically and to unleash the imagination of a larger group in addressing the needs of priests in all stages, from cradle to grave?

Bishops certainly need to see that ongoing formation is offered so that individual priests may grow spiritually and be able to hone their skills, but bishops also need to have at least one team-building event each year for their presbyterates. A presbyteral assembly on the theology of presbyterates is a good beginning. One of the things the business world can teach us here is the difference between task maintenance and group maintenance. The bishop must see to it that individual priests are delivering ministry, but he also needs to pay attention to the cohesiveness of the group delivering the ministry. As the American bishops pointed out so well at the end of *The Basic Plan for the Ongoing Formation of Priests*, "The ongoing formation of individual priests is one thing, but the ongoing formation of presbyterates in their unity is another."

The main task of annual team-building events that focus on group maintenance or team building should initially involve priests writing, adopting and holding each other to a common vision statement. This process might have to start with a few very simple goals and then move gradually toward more complex matters at future team-building events. Without a common vision, small tribes within the presbyterate are left to write their own, sometimes competing, visions. This leads to disunity, infighting and parochialism. In learning how to dialogue with each other, priests could benefit from Pope Paul VI's four points of what he calls the "asceticism of dialogue."[10]

Conclusion

This is only a partial list of the personal and structural changes that priests and bishops must welcome, as well as some of the ideas for implementation they can adopt, to have strong, life-giving and unified presbyterates. In short, priests are facing, at the root of things, a spiritual crisis. The crisis facing presbyterates will be resolved by a spiritual response, not merely a programmatic response. In the end, it is not just a matter of providing the right programs. Only a group change of heart, one priest at a time, will lead to a true renewal of presbyterates. Priests need to take responsibility for their individual spiritual and personal growth, as well as take responsibility for the health of their presbyterates. They must constantly remind themselves and remind each other why they do what they do. When they forget that, their strength is sapped and they soon degenerate into a loose association of "Lone Rangers," leaving individuals isolated and demoralized.

The success of renewing presbyterates and their common sense of purpose rests primarily on enough bishops and priests wanting this unity. Priests need an honest dialogue that will help them recognize what to preserve from the past and what to embrace in the present and into the future. This honest dialogue could lead to developing a new paradigm with workable structures to enable them to offer better service to God's people and be better witnesses to the Gospel. The few essentials are, of course, non-negotiable, but the many incidentals are negotiable. All priests must be able to move from their individual points of view to a common viewing point. From there, they can appreciate not only their own points of view, but also the points of view of others. The church simply cannot afford to have infighting among its priests. Priests owe it to each other, to the next generation of priests and to their people they serve, to become what the church says they are: "intimate sacramental brotherhoods" for a common ministry.

Translating this dream into reality will take great courage. Doubt and laziness are constant enemies. When doubt and laziness reign, there is a strong temptation to let go of part of the dream as a way of resolving inevitable tensions. Success depends on the ability to remain enthusiastic, focused and purposeful to the end. Likewise, the dream of unified presbyterates cannot be accomplished without the graced personal conversion of each and every priest toward his fellow priests. After all, as cited above, *The Basic Plan for the Ongoing Formation of Priests* says quite clearly, "The formation of the presbyterate in its unity is the responsibility of all its members." When it comes to presbyterates, it's way past time to move from neglect to intentionality.

For the vision still has its time, presses on to
fulfillment, and will not disappoint; if it delays, wait
for it, it will surely come, it will not be late.
Habbakuk 2:3

END NOTES

1. Peck, M. Scott, *The Road Less Traveled*, Simon & Schuster, Inc., New York, NY, 1978, pp. 276-277.

2. *Directory for the Life and Ministry of Priests*, No. 27.

3. Drummond, Thomas B., "Sexual Misbehavior and the Infused Competency Myth," The New Life Institute for Human Development Newsletter, The New Life Institute, Middleburg, VA, Winter 2003, Vol. 11, No. 1.

4. Hoge, Dean R., *The First Five Years of the Priesthood*, The Liturgical Press, Collegeville, MN, 2002, p. 101.

5. *The Basic Plan for the Ongoing Formation of Priests*, pp. 95-98.

6. *The Priest and the Third Christian Millennium*, United States Catholic Conference, Washington, DC, 1999, Chapter 4, no. 3.

7. *Origins*, United States Conference of Catholic Bishops, Washington, DC, Vol. 18, no. 31, Jan. 12, 1989.

8. Pope John Paul II, *I Will Give You Shepherds*, St. Paul Books & Media, Boston, MA, 1992, no. 76.

9. Howe, Neil, and William Strauss, *Millennials Rising: The Next Great Generation*, Vintage Books, New York, NY, 2000, pp. 3-29.

10. "Decree on the Bishops' Pastoral Office in the Church," Chapter II, no. 16.

Affecting Change in a Presbyterate: How a Survey of Priests[1] Probed the Attitude for Change in a Presbyterate

Rev. Francis Kelly Scheets, OSC

"No matter what, change always threatens to make matters worse."

What is the issue? In the summer of 2001 I was asked by a friend of mine to join him in checking out the parking lots of a number of Protestant and Catholic parishes. Driving home after this expedition he asked me, "What are they doing that we are not?" Catholic researchers know that "we" are doing the right things — in some parishes. So why not all, or at least in most of them? Affecting change in a presbyterate is complex. We need to know more: what, why, how.

1. Surveying a Presbyterate's Attitude for Change

Why was this presbyterate surveyed? In the spring of 2002, at the height of the clergy sex-abuse scandal, 400 priests of the Archdiocese of Detroit gathered for two "Conversations with the Cardinal." The issues surfacing were many, so the Presbyteral Council favored a survey of the presbyterate, especially of the active clergy, as a way to assess their attitude on a number of statements regarding change. The resolution was approved by Archbishop Adam Cardinal Maida.

I was asked to serve as director of the survey under the directions of an "action-oriented" Survey Committee charged with recommendations. The committee agreed with me that it was important to build our survey around a national survey — if the local clergy were to put adequate "faith" in their own survey. Dr Dean Hoge of Catholic University gave permission to make use of his *Survey of American Priests*[2], conducted in spring of 2001 on behalf of the National Federation of Priests' Councils.

Eight hundred surveys were mailed to active and senior priests of the archdiocese and to those religious community priests assigned to archdiocesan ministries. When the deadline for returns came, I counted 388 responses. I was concerned. Did the active priests scorn this survey?

Did only the senior priests respond? Only weeks later, after the responses were all in the survey database, did I learn that I had an 88% response rate from the priests on active ministry!

Let me share some interesting findings: Their average age was fifty-six. Sixty percent of the priests live alone; about one-fifth are in other ministries than parishes; seventy-one percent have an additional degree beyond the seminary degree with thirty-eight percent having a religious studies degree and thirty-three percent a nontheological or secular degree.

Now to explore the areas in which the presbyterate were tested on their attitude for change.

Did personal issues indicate an "attitude for change"? Hardly. The survey sought responses on their sources of support, satisfaction and frustration — both personal and ministry. I found the priests to be extraordinarily happy! Ninety-two percent agreed or strongly agreed that each "is a happy priest." Eighty-four percent disagreed or strongly disagreed that they even felt like leaving the priesthood. How about that! Now we need to explore the question: Did this general satisfaction reflect other areas of their lives?

Administration of the sacraments and presiding over the liturgy was a "strong" source of ministry support; so responded eighty-three percent while another fourteen percent felt it provided a "somewhat strong" source of ministry support. Other "strong" and "somewhat strong" sources of support surfaced — with scores above eighty percent: preaching the Word, opportunities to exercise one's personal abilities, working with people to share the Good News of the Gospel and being a leader of the Christian community.

Administration skills, nine of them being listed, were a "strong" source of frustration for only six percent and a "somewhat strong" source for nineteen percent. Now note: seventy-five percent of the active priests responded that these skills were "little or no source" or a "mixed or inconsistent source" of frustration.

My Survey Committee raised two questions: Were their parishioners equally satisfied with quality of those liturgies and with their preaching of the Word? Were their staff and parish councils in agreement regarding the adequacy of their administration skills? The committee's recommendations were questioning: "In order to improve on [the] quality ministry a periodic evaluation of parishioners' impressions of the liturgies and homilies" and "a study of the current level of effectiveness of the nine pastoral skills among the presbyterate" seem indicated.

Did institutional issues show an "attitude for change"? Considerably. The survey found: "Strong agreement exists that Vatican II reforms have not gone too far." Eighty-five percent "agreed" or "strongly agreed" that the Vatican II reforms had not gone too far! If that statement does not seem sufficient to support the validity of the statement that the presbyterate favors change, then let me set forth seven other responses.

An impressive ninety-two percent "agreed" or "strongly agreed" that the "presbyterate must incorporate the possibility for continuing change into its life." Further, almost as many agreed that evangelization has to begin at home by "improving the quality of homilies and liturgy." More than seventy percent "agreed" or "strongly agreed": The presbyterate must be willing to take risks, the Church needs to move faster in empowering the laity in ministry, priests need to be more involved with broad social and moral issues, parish life would be aided by a great increase in full-time professional lay ministers, and bishop-priest relationship does not encourage collaboration.

Three statements had more than fifty percent of responses "agree" or "strongly agree" (with about twenty-five percent "uncertain" being a large swing group): There is insufficient collaboration among similar sizes and types of parishes, the election of membership to the councils (presbyterate and vicariate) improves morale[3] and the clergy are not held sufficiently accountable for professional growth.

Did the younger priests also support these statements? A number of the younger priests, those under forty-five years of age, did disagree with their elders regarding the above change statements. Over all, fifty-three percent of the younger priests chose "agree" or "strongly agree" compared with seventy-one percent of the older priests. What did surface was that a fifth of the younger priests were "uncertain" — a large swing group. That "swing" group is yet to be convinced about the need for specific changes.

My Survey Committee and I were impressed with these results. In order to tap this real attitude for change, the committee recommended broad-scale involvement of priests and laity: "Both the Presbyteral Council and the Council of Vicars should make broad use of Task Forces whose membership should involve the presbyterate (and laity) in determination and implementation of policies." In making such a recommendation, the committee prefaced the recommendation: "We think our well-educated presbyterate needs to be a partner in determining and implementing policies" and "We think we must move quickly to increase our professional accountability."

2. Measuring the Real Attitude for Change

Did this presbyterate truly desire change?

We all know that large institutions possess an antipathy to change. Not only is the Catholic Church a large institution, but it is responsible for preserving the legacy of Jesus and the Gospel through the centuries.

How could the presbyterate's *real* attitude for change be determined? I was anxious to test the Detroit priests on their "real" attitude for change, even though I had no idea that the responses to the above eleven statements would suggest so positive an atmosphere for change! To assess their real attitude I needed to be able to compare them to a normal group of persons. Fortunately, sociologists had developed and tested several statements regarding change that would enable me to compare the clergy to a "normal" distribution of individuals.

Let me explain. Research has shown that a sufficiently large group of people fall into a "normal distribution curve." Picture to yourself a hill sloping to the right and to the left. This large hill is divided into two sections — evenly split down the middle with the right side favoring change and the left half opposed. Each half is further split into three sub-groups. Far to the right are smallest number, these are the innovators and the first ones to adopt a new idea. Moving partially up the hill, the next to change are the adopters; this group follows the example of the innovators. The largest segment favoring change, forming up to the crest are the great middle; these are the early majority. Moving to the left of the crest, among those not favoring change is the largest group; they are the late majority. Moving down the hill we find the not-sures[4]; these are the last to accept change. Far to the left are those who resist change forever; these are the not-change group. A "normal distribution curve" has an equal spread on each side of the middle, descending to the extremes, with innovators to the right and not-changers on the left. So much for a normal distribution. (In setting up the survey I combined the two ends: innovators with adopters and the not-sures with the not-change group.)

Did the survey find the presbyterate *really* favored change? No. The survey found the clergy to be less open to change than a normal distribution of individuals. I admit that neither I nor the committee expected a different result.

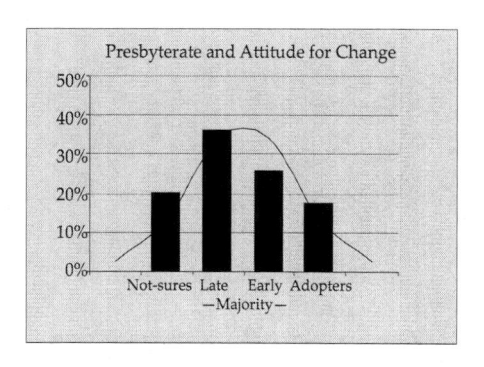

I did find that the adopter-innovators were of a greater percentage than I expected, while the early majority group was well below normal. (See the graph; the black line illustrates the distribution of normal attitudes for change; the bars show the percent of the priests found in the four groups.) The adopter-innovators were twelve percent above average, but the early majority surprised me as this group was twenty-four percent below normal. The late majority were slightly above normal. The not-sures (with the not-change groups), at twenty-six percent above normal, were far more numerous than I expected. The summation of the individual characteristics of all the priests strongly indicates that they would be *really* slow to accept change.

What personal qualities impact their *real* attitude for change? The survey tested seven personal qualities[5] but found that only three affected the overall distribution in change attitudes: education beyond the seminary, year of ordination and whether parish priests had an extra work assignment (e.g. pastor of cluster parishes, teaching, tribunal).

An education degree in addition to the seminary degree proved important. Priests with a non-religious or secular degree and those with a degree in religious studies (e.g. theology, canon law, religious education) were over-represented among the adopter-innovators. It was the priests who did not possess a degree beyond the seminary who were highly over-represented among the not sure-not change priests.

Ordination years proved somewhat significant. I found that the priests ordained during the 1960s were over-represented among the adopter-innovators and among the early majority. The priests ordained before 1960 furnished most of the late majority and the not sure-not change priests.

The Survey Committee, faced with a strong expression for change suggested by the eleven responses I noted above coupled with a majority of the presbyterate (56 %) who are really slower to accept change, recommended: *The Presbyteral Council needs to assure ... special care for its adopters as well as the late majority so that any necessary changes can be experienced in a positive way that does not divide.*

It now remains to explain just why this recommendation called for *special care for its adopters as well as the late majority.*

3. Affecting Change in a Presbyterate

Is there a theory about our attitude for change? Yes. The diffusion of innovation theory was first articulated by Everett M. Rogers of Harvard University in his 1962 study *Diffusion of Innovations*[6]. In that book Rogers developed the concepts to explain how the rate of adoption of a new idea proceeds among those who will benefit from it. He defined this theory: "Diffusion is the process by which an innovation is communicated through certain channels over time among the members of a social system."

Reflect on our experiences with changes in the Catholic Church over the past forty years. That experience has clearly shown all of us two diverse ways for change to happen. Changes mandated by authority come quickly and are explosive! We all bear our scars to the still-ongoing conflicts arising from some of those changes. When changes are left to their "natural course," acceptance takes a generation. To note two "new ideas": parish pastoral councils have been with us for nigh on to thirty years, but still one-fifth of the parishes have yet to institute a council. The RCIA program was started in the early 1980s; today less than one-third of all parishes employ a director.

Why is change so difficult for most people? The diffusion of innovation — the adoption of a new idea — is the study of how knowledge about doing something different is obtained and acted upon. In a word, it is knowing how a group of individuals deal with risk and the uncertainty that accompanies change. I react to change differently than you do, as my willingness to risk is as different as our upbringing and education is varied. We risk leaving the present way of acting worse off for our having tried — if we mess up. We lose the sense of security we derive from knowing that we have done this many times — and that restricts our openness to change. "The new" brings uncertainty, that fear of failure that leads each of us to feel the need to seek social reinforcement in our attitude toward "the new." Only the innovator is willing to risk — alone. Our need for varying degrees of "social reinforcement" is what Everett Rogers studied over forty years ago and what we are going to explore now.

What are the characteristics of "change groups"? Personal, social and educational characteristics are factors related to the speed with which we adopt a new practice or respond to change when first introduced. The characteristics of the earlier groups vary significantly from those of the later groups.

Innovators: The innovators are the most venturesome; they have a large amount of risk capital. They are more literate in that they read books, journals and magazines and may write articles; they have friends in universities and organizations with whom they are in frequent contact. They belong to formal organizations and have many informal contacts; they possess a greater ability to deal with abstractions. They are frequently responsible for larger parishes or occupy responsible positions. Innovators comprise 3% of a group.

Adopters: These adopters have a considerable amount of risk capital; they, too, subscribe to a number of magazines and journals; they, too, participate in the formal activities of organizations. But they tend to wait several years before adopting an idea first developed and used by their innovator friends. Most important, the adopters work out kinks in a new idea and make it adaptable by others so they are trusted by their fellow priests. They, too, are often in charge of the larger parishes or occupy important positions. Adopters comprise 13% of a group. (Together, the innovators and adopters comprise 16%.)

Early Majority: Members of this group possess a moderate amount of risk capital; they read magazines, a few journals and some books. They tend to distrust the innovators among the presbyterate and rely on their friends among the adopters — or among the late majority. They may wait a decade before accepting a new way of doing something and then only after it has proven successful among the adopters. They comprise 34% of a group.

Late Majority: The late majority have a low amount of risk capital and fear that change can only make matters worse. Members of this group read magazines; they seldom attend the activities of regional or national organizations. They distrust the innovators and the adopters to a lesser extent, so they tend to get most of their information from conversations with their friends among the early majority — or among the not-sures. They may wait several decades before committing themselves. They comprise 34% of a group.

Not-Sure and Not-Change: These two categories have very little risk capital and so are suspicious of change. They may wait two or three decades to feel comfortable in adopting a practice — and a number, only when it is mandated by a recognized authority. Change causes a lot of pain and anguish. It is important to understand this group. Don't ignore them, but don't concentrate time, frustration and possible anger on them. Not-sures comprise 13%. (Together with the not-change group they comprise 16%.)

What is necessary to insure a reasonable attitude for change? For each of us, our lived experience is clear. Change is messy, and it takes so-o-o long. It occurs quickly only when a strong authority figure mandates immediate change. In that instance, change is followed by anger and frustration, if not outright rebellion. Why, then, left to itself, must change take twenty to thirty years — a whole generation?

Risk: Change involves risk — a willingness to risk that change will improve upon the presently accepted way. Fear of risk will be reduced only when individuals are aware that the benefits really do exceed the costs.

Skills: Change requires a comfortable level of skill — the "how" to bring "the new" about. The "how" requires many skills: preparing people for change, knowing how to implement change in an orderly manner and how to stabilize "the new" so that it becomes part of the established way of doing things. We should not forget, either, that a given skill may not be easily transferable.

Credibility: Change depends on trust. Trust relates to an individual and not to a group; one trusts one's friends. Those friends are found on either side of the normal curve — an adopter trusts his innovator friends; an early majority trusts his adopter friends; a late majority trusts only his early majority friends; and not-sures hesitate to trust anyone but their friends among the late majority.

I need to state an obvious point: On any one issue, an innovator could easily be among the early majority on another issue. In that case the innovator's level of risk capital may be lower or the needed skills may be non-existent. This survey of priests measured risk and attitude for change in the context of each respondent's general experience.

4. THE UNIQUE CHANGE AGENT: THE PRIEST-ADOPTER

Why protect the *priest-adopter*? Adopters have enough "risk capital" to enable them to undertake something new with confidence following on the initial experience of their innovator friends. The adopter's skills, because he builds on the innovator's success before starting, is able to work out the details and bugs that follow adopting "the new." The adopter reduces the level of risk for the majority because he can measure the success of "the new." Only the adopter inspires credibility among the early majority — and so is trusted much more than the innovators. And what about the late majority? Who is their teacher? It is with their early majority friends that the late majority becomes disposed to accept change.

If the lengthy time lag for effectively implementing something new within a presbyterate is to be shortened, **it is the adopter who must be the teacher!**

If the lengthy time lag for effectively implementing something new within a presbyterate is to be shortened, **it is the early and late majority who must be taught.**

And so it was that the Detroit Survey Committee recommended: *The Presbyteral Council needs to assure ... special care for its adopters as well as the late majority so that any necessary changes can be experienced in a positive way that does not divide.*

How does the adopter become the teacher? Priest adopters need to be made aware of their importance as the teachers to their presbyterate. To make my point, let's take a look at an average diocese: it has 100 parishes ministered to by 106 priests; at the most it may have three innovators and fourteen adopters — and 72 priests scattered between the early and late majorities. Don't overlook the 17 priests among the not sure-not change group. Remember: the few innovators are rarely trusted by the great majority. Innovators possess, to a very high degree, the two qualities needed to accept change — willingness to risk and the skill to bring change about. To the large majority, innovators are not trusted for those very reasons: for them the need for change is unclear, nor do they possess the skill to implement change by themselves. The not-sures and not-change persons are likely to consider innovators as dangerous — destroyers of the proven status quo. The adopters must be the teachers, for they are generally trusted. The adopters must be assured of special care. The late majority need special care — for they have to learn to trust their teachers. To be the teachers, the adopters need a "parish school."

What is this "Parish School"? I would envisage such a school to be in any number of places around the country. I would like to see each attached to a college, university or seminary. I would insist that each school be based on practical learning. My school exists to enable pastors assess the cost-benefits of the risk in change and to assist them in acquiring the needed skills. It should be based on the following three principles.

1: Learning occurs by doing. Participants need to work from prepared case studies that bring out the cost-benefits derived from change or from refusing to change. Participants need to be absorbed with role modeling in order to acquire the skills useful for change. Time — as in weeks — must be allocated for knowledge and transferable skills to be acquired.

2: Learning occurs best among equals. The learning process must occur in a gathering of priests from similar sizes and types of parishes. Sharing must be real to be feasible. Glance back at our average diocese. It has very large parishes — thirty mega-parishes with more than 3,000 registered households — the spiritual home to more than seventy percent of all registered Catholics. The mega-church pastors relate best to other mega-church pastors. Our average diocese has small parishes — thirty-two that register fewer than 1,200 parishioners. Small parish pastors relate best to other small parish pastors. Like relates best to like.

3: Adopters need their skills enhanced. To be effective teachers they have to know how to measure the need for change — how to make use of professional surveys, focus groups. They must know how to obtain comparative before-and-after data — how to measure the benefits of change and its cost. In too many cases, the best of the adopters would need considerable help in developing a good case study. Professional assistance will be needed.

I am not proposing something new. I am only reflecting on what I know of how corporations, banks, government and the military struggle with this same "attitude for change" that the Detroit presbyterate faces. I have long admired Msgr. Philip Murnion's "New Pastors Workshop" — and have attended two. His workshops make use of truly national innovators in order to expose local innovator-adopters to the best practices — but with only four days of lectures. Corporations have come to appreciate the importance of allowing for time — time needed to absorb the case-study approach and of learning among equals.

For more years than I care to acknowledge, I have been haunted by a quote from the management consultant, Peter F. Drucker, that went something like this: "If a corporation has a plant that it cannot prepare its average manager to manage well — it should close the plant." We have not closed the plant, nor have we prepared the average priest to manage well. We have done our clergy a disservice. We failed to provide skills-workshops in which they could learn and practice how to improve preaching[7], liturgies, pastoral council meetings, parish planning, public communication and accountability, and other skills.

Francis Kelly Scheets, OSC, is a member of the Crosier Fathers and Brothers Province. He was director of the Survey of Priests, 2002, for the Presbyteral Council of the Archdiocese of Detroit. He holds a Ph.D. in parish management information systems and is currently working on a book, Catholic Parishes: Challenging the 21st Century.

END NOTES

1 *Survey of Priests, 2002*, © 2003, Archdiocese of Detroit.

2 Hoge, Dean R. and Wenger, Jacqueline E., *Evolving Visions of the Priesthood*; Liturgical Press, St John's Abbey, Collegeville, MN; 2003.

3 The USCCB Committee on Priestly Life and Ministry suggested important changes for improving the morale of priests: election to the presbyterate council, involvement in the determination and implementation of policies, provision of mentors, and frequent contact between the bishop and priests.

4 Laggard is the term generally used; "Not-sures" is a non pejorative term chosen by my Survey Committee.

5 The eight personal qualities were: present age, year of ordination, present assignment, parish location, parish size, non-seminary degree, willing acceptance of change.

6 Rogers, Everett M., *Diffusion of Innovations*, fourth edition; Free Press, Division of Simon & Schuster, Inc., New York, NY; 1995.

7 The Dominicans have been the acknowledged leaders in the improvement of Catholic preaching since Vatican II: the National Institute on the Word of God, the Aquinas Institute's graduate degree program in preaching, homily helps, etc. However, it was Bishop Kenneth Untener of Saginaw, Michigan, who showed us how to improve the quality of preaching among the majority.

The Promise of Obedience of Diocesan Priests

Among the virtues most necessary for the priestly ministry must be that disposition of soul by which priests are always ready to seek not their own will, but the will of the one who sent them.

Obedience is "apostolic" in the sense that it recognizes, loves and serves the Church in her hierarchical structure. Indeed, there can be no genuine priestly ministry except in communion with the supreme pontiff and the episcopal college, especially with one's own diocesan bishop.

Priestly obedience has also a "community" dimension. It is not the obedience of an individual who alone relates to authority, but rather an obedience which is deeply part of the unity of the presbyterate.

This obedience demands a marked spirit of asceticism, both in the sense of a tendency not to become too bound up in one's own preferences or points of view and in the sense of giving brother priests the opportunity to make good use of their talents and abilities, setting aside all forms of jealousy, envy and rivalry. Priestly obedience should be one of solidarity, based on belonging to a single presbyterate. Within the presbyterate, this obedience is expressed in co-responsibility regarding directions to be taken and choices to be made.

Priestly obedience has a "pastoral" character. It is lived in an atmosphere of constant readiness to allow oneself to be taken up, as it were "consumed," by the needs and demands of the flock, especially if they are truly reasonable and genuine.

A summary from
Pastores Dabo Vobis
III, 28

THAT OTHER PROMISE: THE ROLE OF OBEDIENCE IN UNIFIED PRESBYTERATES

Rev. J. Ronald Knott

> *Jesus summoned the twelve and sent them out two by two to preach, drive out demons and cure the sick. Later they gathered together again at a deserted place to rest because things were so busy they had no time to eat. Then James and John made a move for the best seats in the kingdom which caused the other ten to be indignant. Jesus summoned them again and reminded them that true greatness for them was service, not power.*
> Mark 6:7-13, 30-32 and 10:34-45

Working alone, working too much and working against each other have always been the enemies of priests. They are all addressed in these passages from Mark's Gospel. It's worth noting that things have not changed all that much in ministry over the last 2,000 years.

Presbyterates are still plagued with these problems even today, and around the country they are in deep trouble again because of them. These passages present the problem, yes, but they also give us the solution: we are a team; we don't have to do it all ourselves, and we need to support and honor each priest and his gifts. As a presbyterate, we are also a body with many gifted parts like the one Paul talks about, working cohesively under our head, the bishop.

Without each one adding his gifts, doing his part and respecting each other, this body is diminished. This is a living body. It needs constant nurturing or it will get sick and become unable to function. We must constantly confront our loneliness, our stress and our competition or they will kill us.

The priests, who make up the majority of every diocesan presbyterate, make two solemn promises: celibacy and obedience. (It might be good to remind ourselves here that religious priests working under a diocesan bishop are full members of that presbyterate as long as they are working in that diocese. They are not just visitors or mere associates.)

Rather than negatives, the promises of celibacy and obedience are meant to free us up for ministry. Celibacy makes it possible for us to become that "intimate sacramental brotherhood for the purpose of ministry" that the Church speaks about.

Of the two promises, the only one we ever hear much about, after we make it, is celibacy. We never hear too much about "the other promise," the promise of obedience. It, too, makes it possible for us to be that "intimate sacramental brotherhood for the purpose of ministry."

The older I get, the more I appreciate the wisdom of our two promises. Regardless of all the pious exaggeration written about the beauties of celibacy, I agree that, if embraced and lived freely, it can be freeing. It can free one up for a greater good, for full-time service to the People of God. The only time I have ever thought much about obedience, or needed to, was when I got my first assignment after I was ordained.

As one who was born in the country but urbanized quite well by the seminary system, I had my heart set on being an associate pastor in a large suburban parish in Louisville, where restaurants, theaters and friends were all around. What I got was an assignment to the "home missions" of our diocese, on the edge of Appalachia, a parish the size of the state of Delaware with a Catholic population of one tenth of one percent, as far away from Louisville as one could get. My family and friends were three hours away.

I cried, I pleaded and I even took to my bed — to no avail! I had to go "out of obedience." I was a bit like those people who join the National Guard in peacetime, not imagining that they would ever have to fight a war. I balked at first, but with God's help, I was able to turn my mind around.

Since I didn't get what I wanted, I decided to want what I got. That, I believe, is part of the true spirit behind the "promise of obedience." I went because the bishop has the "big picture" and said he needed me there. I went because I promised him and his successors that I would go where the Church needed my gifts.

Yes, I was upset and disappointed. Yes, I tried to change his mind, but in the end, I knew that it was me who needed to change my mind. I did change it, not grudgingly, but with as much good spirit as I could muster. (By the way, that assignment turned out to be fabulous, one that led directly to later assignments that were all the loves of my life.)

Over the years, my understanding and appreciation of "obedience" has evolved. It has matured. I have come to see that the "promise of obedience" has implications beyond the person of the bishop. It includes a promise to fellow members of my presbyterate. Rather than making me a slave to the whims of one particular person, the bishop, it is really a promise to be a "team player" with the bishop and the other members of my presbyterate for the sake of the common purpose we share: effective ministry to the People of God. It is this understanding of the "promise of obedience," a promise to be a "team player," that I believe will lead to a renewal of our presbyterates. The theology is quite clear: we are not priests, one by one. We are priests in a presbyterate under a bishop. "Lone rangers" and "priests in private practice" are heretical!

Remember these promises? You made them! I made them! We meant them, didn't we? Didn't we? (1) "Are you resolved, with the help of the Holy Spirit, to discharge without fail the office of the priesthood in the presbyteral order as a conscientious fellow worker with the bishops in caring for the Lord's flock?" (2) "Do you promise respect and obedience to me and my successors?" How do those promises sound to you after all these years? How do they sound today as we prepare to let go of the bishop we have known and accept a yet-unknown new bishop?

Priests do not carry out their own ministry; they are fellow workers in helping the bishop carry out his ministry. For the bishop to carry out his ministry of caring for the Lord's flock, his team of fellow workers must be on the same page with him. That is why respect and obedience is needed! All this is beautifully put in Eucharistic Prayer I for Masses of Reconciliation: "Keep us all in communion of mind and heart with our Pope and our bishop."

At a time when we need to work together as a team, we seem to be growing further and further apart. As Lily Tomlin would put it, "We are all in this together, by ourselves." A new look at, and a new appreciation of, our promise of obedience, I believe, can be the beginning of the reversal of that trend.

An expansive understanding of "promise of obedience" is the only thing we have in our arsenal as diocesan priests to ritualize that group resolve because, in it, we promise each other to be "team players." We cannot have a healthy, unified presbyterate when everyone is self-focused. We are an orchestra, not a loose association of soloists. We are one body with many parts, each with gifts the whole body needs. Like the original twelve, Christ calls us to resist those things that threaten this unity, especially working alone, working too much and working against each other.

Brother priests! In a nutshell, I believe with all my heart that what is needed most of all is to move from our various points of view to a viewing point where we can appreciate each other's point of view as well as our own, a one-priest-at-a-time conversion, away from an exaggerated good of the individual to the good of the group, for the sake of effective ministry to the People of God. The only public expression of that conversion is our promise to each other, through our leader, to be "team players." We need to revisit our "promise of obedience." We need, I believe, to remind ourselves, regularly and in the most dramatic way possible, what we have committed ourselves to be: "fellow workers with the bishop in caring for the Lord's flock." It is so easy to forget that we do not carry out our own ministry, but that of the bishop. We are his ministry team, and for the sake of his coherent ministry, we are called to set our differences aside and work as a cohesive unit for the sake of God's people.

Let us take ourselves back to our original enthusiasm. Let us reclaim and renew our promise of obedience, a promise to be a team player in our ministry to the People of God, with our bishop and with each other.

© *2010 Our Sunday Visitor, Inc. All rights reserved. No permission required for reprint.*

CHAPTER 2

THE MINISTRY OF UNITY

AT ODDS WITH OURSELVES: POLARIZATION AND THE LEARNING CULTURES OF PRIESTHOOD

David B. Couturier, OFM Cap

In his most recent book, *A People Adrift*, Peter Steinfels makes the claim that the Catholic Church in America is "polarized and beset by acrimony and suspicion," with conservatives regularly accusing liberals of heresy and liberals often charging conservatives with abandoning the Gospel.[1] Dean Hoge, in a recent survey of trends in the priesthood, finds that priests are interpreting the conditions of the church in vastly different ways, leading to a growing polarization among older and younger clergy.[2] Why is the laity polarized, and why is the priesthood increasingly at odds with itself?

Steinfels roots the problem in narrative interpretations that he finds outdated and inadequate. Clergy and laity love the same church and experience the same challenges. They are divided, however, by two frames of reference, two interpretive schemes, that draw their energy from each other's fault lines, progressive on the one hand and traditionalist on the other. Steinfels, like many others, sees the state of the church as an ideological tug of war with two opposing sides.

Unfortunately, the situation is more complex. In this article, I will argue three points: 1) The polarization in the priesthood is not a function of identity confusion as much as it is the result of the reinvention of pastoral service. 2) There are now seven narratives or "interpretive schemes" that help priests and laity make sense of their Catholic world. 3) Seminaries must help seminarians negotiate, not abandon, this diversity so that they can recognize and advance the fullness of Catholic life in an increasingly international and globalized world.

The Reinvention of Pastoral Service

There are many reasons why dedicated and well-motivated members of a group turn their frustration on one another.[3] Confusion about one's identity is only one of them. Besides this, organizational psychologists tell us that changes in work and service, especially if unforeseen and ill prepared for, will produce anxiety in the community, which the group will try to manage by primitive processes of scapegoating and projection.[4]

Facing difficult changes, the group will psychologically split itself into the "good guys" and the "bad guys," those who are faithful and those who are not. These ideological splits take on a life of their own, with participants truly believing that they are fighting a battle over beliefs and values. While members of the group actually agree more than they disagree, these skirmishes serve as containers for the group's anxiety. They become chronic social defense mechanisms when group members fail to recognize the true source of their anxiety: how difficult work has become and how uneasy they feel when they are unsure about their effectiveness.

This is, I believe, the situation of priesthood and religious life today. The ministerial landscape of the church continues to change in dramatic ways. There have already been critical changes in ministerial partnerships, priorities, world views and perceptions.[5] Catholic parishes are moving from the organizational dynamics associated with institutions of single interest to those associated with institutions of multiple interests. The once largely clericalized system of ministerial leadership has opened (to some degree) to new partnerships (largely with women), new priorities (beyond the confines of its early immigrant history) and new world views (that encompass the religious needs of an increasingly more complex and diversified spectrum of Catholic cultures and community).

But, time and experience indicate how challenging this project truly is. Balancing the needs, expectations and concerns of a new class of lay professional ministers, especially men and women of color, is a task largely unfulfilled for two reasons. First, these dedicated lay ministers have so little0 power with which to influence the critical priorities of diocesan life. Second, the increasing economic vulnerability of American parishes further threatens the security and status of these lay ministers. So, too, does their inability to develop a stronger network of influence in chanceries that are slow to reflect the racial, cultural and gender diversity of American Catholic life.

Ministry has become even more complex and stressful. According to a recent study by priest sociologist John H. Morgan, the average Catholic priest works 60 to 70 hours per week on ministry.[6] That number is sure to climb, since priests have inherited two kinds of pastoral planning strategies that cannot adequately address both the organizational and the spiritual challenges facing a growing and complex church community. The first strategy from the period of Catholic expansion (1850-1950) emphasized hierarchical control, top-down management, uniformity of purpose and a clearly defined but limited sense of mission. The second and more recent strategy is a model of diminishment that is characterized by downsizing, the merging and yoking of parishes, doing more with less and the emergence of forced choices between key pastoral values.[7]

In the organizational psychology of diminishment, an increasingly older clergy is expected to do more with less. Retirement ages are increased to hold on to the last large cohort of priestly workers. Active priests are expected to work longer and harder. Seminarians are prepared to pastor two, three or four parishes simultaneously and to do so with the attitude of a man set apart."[8]

"While the rhetoric of polarization is ideological, the origins of it are decidedly organizational. The reinvention of pastoral service in American Catholic life needs a language and a method that adequately reflect the institutional shifts going on. The interpretive schemes of the "progressive" and "traditionalist" are indeed inadequate for the task.

American Catholics stand in a different place with a different set of needs. The globalized and diversified world of the 21st century calls us to move from the "parochial culture" of the 20th century to the "international mission culture" of the 21st. The largely local, ethnic and neighborhood concerns of the past have to be supplemented with an active and effective ethic for the plight of our sisters and brothers around the world.[9] As parishes move out even farther from their ethnic origins, they will be challenged to develop partnerships and priorities with churches, communities, civic groups and other institutions of good will with differing points of view and methodologies of service. Parishes could be revealed as one of the most effective intersections between local issues and international economic policies and social practices. This development will further challenge the traditional understanding of the local community's task, role and authority. Those challenges will have a distinctively organizational feel to them.

Priests will not be able to manage this transition alone. Therefore, it must be a matter of some concern when a recent survey finds dramatic differences between diocesan and religious clergy on the importance of collaboration with the laity and the participation of women in ministry.[10] It is also critical that the laity on whom we have recently depended may now be increasingly out of reach for ministerial service. This is so because Americans are working differently, and there has been and continues to be a fundamental reorganization and re-imagining of what it means to labor and to serve in Western culture. A recent study from the Economic Policy Institute showed that the average middle-class mother and father are working an extra 6 weeks per year (an extra 246 hours) since 1989.[11] This means the laity have less time with children and less time with parents, friends and neighbors in need. It suggests less time available for volunteerism, charity work and religion.

Even as American Catholics are more educated and interested in the ministries of the church, they are finding themselves increasingly isolated from the opportunities to serve because of the encroaching economic requirements of American life.

Under all these organizational conditions, polarization serves a socially defensive function of containing group anxiety. Unfortunately, the institutional anxiety of the Catholic Church is further contained by seven narratives, or lenses, by which priests (and now their people) interpret their Catholic lives and order their behavior. These are the learning cultures of priesthood.

The Learning Cultures of Priesthood

When we apply the term "culture" to a religious institution, we refer to the community's shared and coherent way of interpreting its world. We are pointing to the complex system of "interpretive schemes" that we have developed over time to make sense of and learn about our worlds. These are our collective assumptions about why events happen as they do and how people act in different situations.

Although some researchers have pointed to various "models" or "conceptions" of formation, these do not go far enough in describing the non-rational learning impact of a seminary's organizational rituals and emotions at both the formal and informal levels.[12]

An organizational cultural system has four ingredients: 1) Beliefs, a shared conceptual understanding of what and how things are; 2) Rituals, patterns of action and practice; 3) Artifacts, distinctive tools or instruments for action; and 4) Affects, patterns of emotion that guide appropriate behavior in the group. A Catholic group (such as a seminary) reflects these cultural patterns both formally in its documents (such as a mission statement or catalogue) and informally by way of anecdotal history, group stories and community practices that are not written down but are affectively normative, nonetheless.

There are, I believe, seven learning cultures in priesthood today. These diverse patterns of understanding, emotions, rituals and tools help seminarians and priests mediate their world, interpret their experiences and make decisions as to appropriate action. They are the models that seminarians and priests use (individually and corporately) for acting in the world, learning from its challenges and creating the social realities that will make up their future.

Each of these seven learning cultures applies different learning tools to the practice of religious living. The learning tools used by different groups in religion, including the books read, the workshops attended and the religious language preferred, all reinforce inherited cultural beliefs. They form a continuous loop of interaction between what priests believe and what they expect, what they presently understand and what they decide are appropriate for further analysis.

These learning cultures originated in seminary and religious formation programs. They are now the learning fields from which seminarians come and to which they will return after ordination.

This diversity of learning cultures offers priestly life a richness of perspective not apparent just a generation ago. At the same time, it offers the potential for misinterpretation and polarization.

1. THE ESSENTIALIST CULTURE.

Men trained in an essentialist culture were taught and continue to maintain that the primary task of priestly life is the personal sanctification of their souls and the faithful transmission of the essential principles of Christian doctrine. Their language is apologetic, and they consider their primary theological responsibility to be a faithful transmission of tradition, especially as this has been handed down in the formulae of the neo-scholastic school of thought.

There is a specific didactic and hierarchical learning style to this culture. Values are learned through externally imposed habits. Devotional practices strongly influence their prayer forms. Those who share this culture are very loyal to the institution of the church. Because of their apologetic stance, they value docility and clarity of thought.

Because of their perspective of a church on the defensive and the need to counteract a secular world view, men trained in this period emphasize the importance of obedience and allegiance to higher authority. They regularly refer to the priority "objective truth." Their rituals and language are rooted in a much larger discourse about our place in the "order of perfection."

Essentialists learned their lessons about order, precedence, sacrifice, discipline and self-control in the food rituals and body disciplines of their early training. Priests in an essentialist culture learned that the universe was marvelously designed and all creatures are hierarchically ordered one to the other (some naturally higher than others). They have come to respect order and expect it. The structures of church communities ought to reflect and adhere, they believe, to such obvious and eternal truths.

At their best, these "loyal bearers of tradition" remind the community of the importance of unity and the continuity of faith so necessary for a community's transmission of Gospel witness. They challenge all of us to clarity of mind, thought and will. At their worst, however, their learning can be limited by an idiosyncratic rendering of papal fundamentalism that lacks theological depth, social context or historical criticism.

These men have distinct learning preferences. At assemblies and retreats these men expect to hear an explicit rendering of "what the church says" and what it wants as a necessary preamble for any further discussion. By that they mean the clear and concise directives of the magisterium. They define obediential discernment and proper religious learning within the tightly packaged parameters of an ordered universe. Clearly, authority and reverential learning come from above. They are not used to and often seem uncomfortable in the messy world of "dialogue" and "shared faith." They will generously attend large or small group meetings out of immense loyalty to the institution, but they find group discussions untidy, disruptive, rambling and chaotic. While they enjoy the spirit of community developed at these gatherings, they do not expect to learn much from these horizontal initiatives.

The popularity of EWTN signals how strong this learning culture still is in Catholic religious circles. For all the criticisms leveled against her, Mother Angelica has shown that one can take an essentialist culture of learning and translate it into the modern medium of a global television network.

2. THE EXISTENTIALIST CULTURE.

The primary goal of this culture is not the transmission of objective knowledge so much as it is the personal development of human and spiritual maturity. This culture was influenced by the council's anthropological "turn toward the subject" and the developmental view of the church as "the people of God."

This emphasis on the subject of formation encouraged new learning initiatives as religious directors and the faculty of seminaries expanded their roles as professors and became formation advisors to those entering seminary formation. Techniques from counseling psychology were imported into formational practice in order to accelerate the personal learning of seminarians as holy and mature men.

Individuals were now being encouraged to become self-reflective learners. Today, they value sincerity, personal growth and authenticity as starting points for a mature discussion of church matters. They measure their own learning by testing challenges against the range of their experiences. Unlike their predecessors, they are less inclined to rely on the test of past generations and almost never find a documented text the sole basis for arguing or winning a point.

This group feels more comfortable at assemblies and meetings than their predecessors, especially if they can "tell their stories." Their commitment to authenticity allows them to track personal learning through honest and shared reflection of religious experiences. The value they place on personal responsibility invites every member of the community to a similar ownership and individual learning. This group has fought long and hard to develop a foundation for personal maturity and to build a spiritual life rooted in a secure personal understanding and appropriation of the implications of Gospel living.

If there is a weakness to this culture, it is that there is often little awareness or patience for the development of a shared vision and a mutual responsibility for the future of the institution or community. A common heritage is more likely assumed than nurtured by members of this group. Personal meaning and individual learning are such hard-won achievements that this group may fail to appreciate the importance of organizational learning and shared understanding. They often seem terrified by the threat of a return to groupthink.

Because it is enough for them that each individual finds his or her own way, members of this culture fail to realize how foundational group experience is. They rarely attend to the structural or organizational dimensions of living. Their exclusive concentration on individual needs keeps them from seeing and learning from the social context and direction of those needs.

3. The Socialization Culture.

The atmosphere of learning changed during the era of the socialization culture. We divided religious buildings and seminaries, once monolithic structures, into sections. Groups of seminarians or religious met for "corridor Masses." Wings of the house often had quiet rooms where small groups could meet for common prayer and informal faith sharing.

Religious learning took another form. This is seen in the developing roles of formation personnel. In the essentialist era, formation directors were professors who taught courses such as the essential principles of the spiritual life. They were replaced in the existentialist period by formation directors who developed one-on-one formation counseling sessions with individuals. Seminaries developed formation teams who helped shape new communities of religious practice.

Great emphasis would be placed on the promotion of community and the spirit of brotherhood in the seminary. Some of this was in reaction to the highly individualized era that preceded it. Mostly it reflected the realization that discernment and religious learning were a communal act of faith and that councils and dialogue provided a new and exciting way to learn about God's will.

Today, men trained in this culture enter the learning environment with the expectation that the first step towards any authentic spiritual growth is not personal insight but the development of the bond between members of the community. We learn best, they believe, when we are in healthy relationships. Religious learning is not only an individual enterprise, it is eminently a social event.

Men in this culture expect to develop a healthy relationship in the community so that they can exercise a proper discernment of spirits in the group. For them, relationships are not automatic and cannot be presumed.

They are unlike the essentialists who learn God's designs almost exclusively through authority figures and the apparently ordered patterns of the universe. Unlike the existentialists for whom religious learning occurs in the dynamics of mature individual conscience formation, these men learn through the practices and rituals that build a shared commitment base. They are enlivened and transformed by the power of dialogue and the mutual sharing of ideas. To them the climate of the essentialist world is too ideal, constricted, ordered and manufactured for ready and easy results. At the same time, the existentialist world with its repetitive challenges to autonomy and freedom of choice seems too isolated, competitive and self-absorbed.

4. The Behavioral Culture.

Men trained in this culture have a more practical, action-oriented, "just do it" mentality. They want results and are more inclined to ask about goals and objectives than about attitudes and motivations. They learn more from watching people's actions than listening to people's explanations.

This culture tires easily of prescriptions and promises; it wants deeds. If analysis is needed, they will trust scientific surveys before they will trust individual impressions and group discussions. They see behaviorally based instruments as more economical ways to get beyond the endless "whys" of religious dynamics.

Religious learning is not assured by a simple compliance of individuals to the wishes of authority figures nor is it derived from personally "authentic" experiences. Learning does not happen by group consensus. The behaviorist is too suspicious of the artificial manufacturing of social bonds. Religious learning, for the behaviorist, is the result of rigorous and consistent research into and the applications of the actions of religious individuals and groups.

5. The Neo-Essentialist Culture.

This is one of the most popular new learning cultures in seminaries today. Although men in this culture look like their essentialist counterparts, there are important differences. They, too, like the clear principles and order of the essentialist culture. No wonder! Their early experiences of church were filled with learning experiences that appeared to them as if "anything goes." They often tell stories of liturgical celebrations or religious classes from their youth where surprise and spontaneity were the order of the day.

Combined with their social experiences of divorce, separation and cultural scandals, these men long for, and sometimes demand, containment for their social anxieties. Because of this, they find the existentialist learning environment ineffective in addressing the social and cultural challenges they face. Immediate immersion into the socialization environment, so often expected of these men in religious settings, is frankly too emotionally difficult to sustain over time. While these men have inherited the languages of these two previous cultures, they have not necessarily learned their skills.

Today they value discipline and emphasize the importance of strong leadership. They want a safe, recuperative learning style that is more directive than experiential. These men appear principled and sure about what they expect from the church. However, they are different from their predecessors.

They lack the familial, social and religious bonding that their elders could take for granted. They have experienced more unprocessed family pain and witnessed more social disruption than their essentialist elders are willing to admit. This causes considerable anxiety in these young people and explains, at least in part, their sometimes severe reactions. It also helps us understand their unusual dilemma. While they are often quite sure about what they want others to do and abide by, they also can be quite flexible as to what they wish to commit themselves to for the long haul. This gives them a unique and paradoxical quality: strong institutional values with a flexible self-discipline.

6. The Liberation Culture.

Men trained in this culture begin with a preferential option for the poor. They see the primary task of evangelization to be the work of liberation and the inclusion of God's poor at the common table of creation and redemption. They are more likely than their predecessors to be critical of unjust structures in society and the church. This is so because their learning begins with the lived experience of those who are suffering. The text they read (and they read it religiously) is the enormous suffering erupting in the post-modern world of competitive capitalism.

These men place great emphasis on developing a critical social analysis of the conditions giving rise to unfair practices within a community. In church discussions, they will often advance the language and practices of inclusion and frame their concerns in the language of human rights and social justice.

Their rituals, beliefs, emotions, and practices center around their unifying principle: God hears the cry of the poor. They expect action on behalf of those unfairly treated as a precondition for (and not just as a consequence of) the dialogue of faith. This stance puts them in a different learning space than the other cultures of priesthood. Discussions that are not directly focused on structural conversion or linked to the practice of justice leave many in this group feeling disenfranchised and lost. More than that, it leaves them feeling irresponsible and like "unjust stewards" in the face of enormous human suffering.

7. THE PROFESSIONAL CULTURE.

There has emerged a new class of entrants who come with a distinct set of dynamics. These are men who enter with established careers and informed adult life choices. Unlike previous generations of priests, they come with an adult (not adolescent) identity, secure careers, a network of social bonds, a history of social and financial obligations, and a learning style derived from the organizational dynamics of a contemporary corporate world.

This is the first generation of seminarians who do not forge their adult identities and social bonds within the religious community but come with adult responsibilities already secured. Some have been married; others have a history of mortgages. They come with a history of supervisory relationships that imply a unique and contemporary understanding of how adults negotiate task, role and authority in a post-modern world.

Learning in the modern workplace from which these men come is vastly different from the learning of all other religious cultures. For those coming from the corporate world, cross-functional teamwork already has replaced traditional hierarchy. Individual initiative and creativity, once discouraged in seminaries, are now highly prized. Since companies no longer guarantee careers, only opportunities, these men have learned that professional entrepreneurship is an essential and expected practice of vocational learning.

Men trained in a global work culture of mutual accountability and transparency do not expect directives and orders from above or vague challenges to authenticity and freedom. They come from work cultures where one earns respect for one's expertise and influence. They are often shocked by religious cultures that demand preferences based on status alone. With extensive experience and sensitivity to the ethics and politics of harassment, they balk at the sometimes intrusive (and non-credentialed) counseling techniques of well-meaning but untrained existentialist directors who "want to get to know" the personal lives of their charges.

"Professional" seminarians, with their sensitivity to the precision of organizational development, are critical of what appear to be arbitrary or confusing standards of formation manuals. Coming from a corporate world of employment with sometimes vast, interlocking and virtual information networks and cross-functional teams, these men find themselves strikingly alone in religious programs. Their corporate learning environments were often fast-paced, multi-centered, culturally and ethnically diverse, demanding provocative engagement. Their new religious learning environments can be monochrome, culturally uniform, and lack the intellectual and social stimulation to which they have become accustomed.

SEMINARIES AND THE LEARNING CULTURES OF PRIESTHOOD

Seminaries have two obligations as we go forward. First, they must provide seminarians with the skills, language and methods needed to manage the increasingly structural and organizational dynamics of Catholic life. Structural conversion must take its place alongside the methods of personal, interpersonal and ecclesial conversion already being taught in the seminary system.

Second, seminarians must be helped to understand and respect the diverse learning cultures of ecclesial life. They are vastly different ways by which priests (and now laity) interpret and constitute their congregational realities. Priests and laity today are likely to see and feel the world in contrasting ways and to respond to its challenges according to the actions, artifacts (literature), emotions and beliefs consistent with their inherited learning culture.

Seminarians and priests must be helped to negotiate the transitions that will be expected of them as they move in and out of these various cultural forms. Modern parishes now reflect the influence of these varying cultures of formation. Seminarians should be able to identify their own preferred learning culture and respectfully engage the needs and assumptions of the others. This diversity of learning cultures gives the church today one of its most original and potentially beneficial experiences of ministry. Each of these cultures highlights an important dimension of evangelization: unity, maturity, community, action, leadership, justice and creativity.

These inherited cognitive and effective learning patterns are not easily changed, but they can be effectively managed to provide a richer and more nuanced perspective on mission and evangelization in the twenty-first century. In the end, polarization is serving as a social defense against the rich diversity of contemporary Catholic life.

David B. Couturier, OFM Cap, is presently vicar provincial and director of formation for the New York-New England Capuchins. He is the founding director of The Center for Structural Conversion, an organizational development consultation service for religious communities. Dave has taught at St. Bonaventure University and the North American College in Rome. He holds a doctorate in pastoral counseling.

END NOTES

1. Peter Steinfels, *A People Adrift* (New York: Simon and Schuster, 2003).

2. Dean R. Hoge, "Recent Research Findings Pertaining to Formation of Religious Priests," unpublished manuscript (Conference on Formation for Celibacy, Jacksonville, FL, December 2002).

3. Larry Hirschhorn, *Reworking Authority: Leading and Following in the Post-Modern Organization* (Cambridge, MA: The MIT Press, 1997).

4. William M. Czander, *The Psychodynamics of Work and Organizations* (New York: Guilford Press, 1993) and Larry Hirschhorn, *The Workplace Within: The Psychodynamics of Organizational Life* (Cambridge, MA: The MIT Press, 1988).

5. I treat these issues at length in David B. Couturier, "The Reinvention of Work in Religious Communities of Men," *New Theology Review* 11:3 (August 1998), pp. 22-35.

6. John H. Morgan, Scholar, Priest and Pastor: Priorities among Clergy Today (Donaldson, IN: Graduate Theological Foundations, 1998).

7. David B. Couturier, "Repairing the Church: Enlivening our Communion as Prophetic Witness in a Troubled Church," July 2003.

8. For an analysis of this attitude of a "man set apart," cf. Hoge, op. cit.

9. David B. Couturier, "Prophetic Preaching after a War," *Touchstone* 18:1 (September 2003).

10. Cf. Hoge, op. cit.

11. Lawrence Mishel, Jared Bernstein, and Heather Boushey, "The State of Working America 2002-2003" (Economic Policy Institute: www.epinet.org, 2002). The text indicates that the average two-parent family now works a full 16 more weeks than it did in 1979.

12. Martin O'Reilly presents helpful insights into these early models in "Current Conceptions of Religious Formation," *Review for Religious* 44:6 (Nov./Dec. 1985), pp. 801-807.

Reprinted with permission from the NCEA Seminary Department. This article first appeared in Seminary Journal, *Volume 9 No. 3 (Winter 2003).*

Civil Discourse: Speaking the Truth with Respect

Donald Cardinal Wuerl
Archbishop of Washington

The preacher's pulpit, the politician's podium, and the print and electronic media all bear some responsibility to encourage a far more civil, responsible and respectful approach to national debate and the discussion of issues in our country today.

Over and over again, we are hearing, in the wake of the shooting of Representative Gabrielle Giffords, that it is time to examine the tenor and tone of debate. Sadly, it took something as tragic as the Tucson shooting to generate a conversation about how we debate issues, especially those that engender great emotion.

A wise and ancient Catholic maxim has always insisted that we are to "hate the sin and love the sinner." At the heart of this time-honored wisdom is the simple recognition that some things are wrong, and yet we still distinguish between what is done and who does it.

Increasingly, there is a tendency to disparage the name and reputation, the character and life, of a person because he or she holds a different position. The identifying of some people as "bigots" and "hate mongers" simply because they hold a position contrary to another's has unfortunately become all too commonplace today. Locally, we have witnessed rhetorical hyperbole that, I believe, long since crossed the line between reasoned discourse and irresponsible demagoguery.

It should not be acceptable to denounce someone who favors immigration reform that includes the process to citizenship as a "traitor" and "unpatriotic." The representatives in federal and state government who voted against the District of Columbia Opportunity Scholarship Program or against tax credits for Catholic schools educating minority children should not be labeled in the media as "anti-

Catholic bigots" or "racists" since the majority of the children are African American. People and organizations should not be denounced disparagingly as "homophobic" simply because they support the traditional, worldwide, time-honored definition of marriage. The defaming words speak more about political posturing than about reasoned discourse.

Why is it so important that we respect both our constitutional right to free speech and our moral obligation that we not bear false witness against another? A profoundly basic reason is that we do not live alone. While each of us can claim a unique identity, we are, nonetheless, called to live out our lives in relationship with others — in some form of community.

All human community is rooted in this deep stirring of God's created plan within us that brings us into ever-widening circles of relationship: first with our parents, then our family, the Church and a variety of community experiences, educational, economic, cultural, social and, of course, political. We are, by nature, social and tend to come together so that in the various communities of which we are a part, we can experience full human development. All of this is part of God's plan initiated in creation and reflected in the natural law that calls us to live in community.

What does this have to do with toning down our rhetoric? Everything! No community, human or divine, political or religious, can exist without trust. At the very core of all human relations is the confidence that members speak the truth to each other. It is for this reason that God explicitly protected the bonds of community by prohibiting falsehood as a grave attack on the human spirit. "You shall not bear false witness against your neighbor" (Ex 20:16). To tamper with the truth or, worse yet, to pervert it, is to undermine the foundations of human community and to begin to cut the threads that weave us into a coherent human family.

To speak the truth requires personal self-discipline and conscious effort. We must search out the facts and avail ourselves of the information necessary to make a judgment based on truth. It is a disservice to the truth when one's opinions, positions or proposals are based on unverified gossip, unsupported rumor or partial information, when all the facts are readily available to us. Serious research and study are demanded in serious matters.

The call to truthfulness is far from being a denial of freedom of speech. Rather, it is a God-given obligation to respect the very function of human speech. We are not free to say whatever we want about another, but only what is true. To the extent that freedom is improperly used to sever the bonds of trust that bind us together as a people, to that extent it is irresponsible. The commandment that obliges us to avoid false witness also calls us to tell the truth.

Someone once described a "gossip" as a person who will never tell a lie if a half-truth will do as much harm. When we listen to news accounts or read what is presented in the print and electronic media, we are too often reminded that spin, selecting only some of the facts, highlighting only parts of the picture, has replaced an effort to present the facts — the full story. We all know the tragic results of gossip against which there is little or no defense. In an age of blogs, even the wildest accusations can quickly become "fact." Gossip is like an insidious infection that spreads sickness throughout the body. These untruths go unchallenged because the persons who are the object of the discussion are usually not present to defend themselves, their views or their actions.

Irresponsible blogs, electronic and print media stories, and pulpit and podium people-bashing rhetoric can be likened to many forms of anonymous violence. Spin and extremist language should not be embraced as the best this country is capable of achieving. Selecting only some facts, choosing inflammatory words, spinning the story are activities that seem much more directed to achieving someone's political purpose rather than reporting events. We have all seen examples of this. One side in a discussion is described as "an inquiring mind that simply wants to know" and the other side is depicted as "lashing out in response."

We need to look at how we engage in discourse and how we live out our commitment to be a people of profound respect for the truth and our right to express our thoughts, opinions and positions — always in love. We who follow Christ must not only speak the truth but must do so in love (Eph 4:15). It is not enough that we know or believe something to be true. We must express that truth in charity with respect for others so that the bonds between us can be strengthened in building up the body of Christ.

Each of us is a temple of the Holy Spirit. Our Baptism into Christ creates among us the bonds of a new spiritual family life. Within this family, each person must ensure that the dialogue proceeds in a manner that not only achieves the ends desired but also recognizes everyone's rights. It would be a true tragedy to accept as a principle of discourse that the end justifies the means so that "winning" would validate any destructive behavior or speech. While each person engaged in discourse is understandably concerned about his or her point of view, the rights of others, including the claims of truth itself, cannot be forgotten. At no time is the spiritual violence of falsehood an acceptable component of Christian discourse.

The *Catechism of the Catholic Church* (2478) quotes Saint Ignatius of Loyola and his spiritual exercises when speaking about Christian discourse: "Every good Christian ought to be more ready to give a favorable interpretation to another's statement than to condemn it. But if he cannot do so, let him ask how the other understands it. And if the latter understands it badly, let the former correct him with love."

We Catholics need regularly to reflect on how we engage in discourse and how we live out our commitment as members of the Church, people with profound respect for the truth and a family of faith committed to expressing our thoughts, opinions and positions always in love. We must also consider how one responds to decisions made for the good of the Church with which a person may disagree.

Even while there may be disagreements within the ecclesial community on policies and procedures, there is a presupposition that we are all one in our faith. One of the reasons why we should find it easy as a Church to arrive at consensus is because it is Christ who calls us together in the first place. Even if we do disagree on some particular practical issue, we must always do so in love.

Basic to Christian discourse is the belief that truth itself is strong enough to win the day. It rejects the maxim, "the one who yells the loudest wins." All have a right to voice their opinions, but it is the truth that should direct the discussion and ultimately prevail.

Freedom of speech and respect for others, freedom of expression and regard for the truth should always be woven together. This should be true of everyone, whether they speak from a pulpit, a political platform, or through the electronic and print media and other means of social communications.

Originally published as a two-part commentary in the Washington Standard *on February 3 and 10, 2011. Reprinted with permission.*

THE PROPER CHARACTERISTICS OF DIALOGUE

Pope Paul VI

81. Dialogue, therefore, is a recognized method of the apostolate. It is a way of making spiritual contact. It should, however, have the following characteristics:

1) Clarity before all else; the dialogue demands that what is said should be intelligible. We can think of it as a kind of thought transfusion. It is an invitation to the exercise and development of the highest spiritual and mental powers a man possesses. This fact alone would suffice to make such dialogue rank among the greatest manifestations of human activity and culture. In order to satisfy this first requirement, all of us who feel the spur of the apostolate should examine closely the kind of speech we use. Is it easy to understand? Can it be grasped by ordinary people? Is it current idiom?

2) Our dialogue must be accompanied by that meekness which Christ bade us learn from Himself: "Learn of me, for I am meek and humble of heart." (56) It would indeed be a disgrace if our dialogue were marked by arrogance, the use of bared words or offensive bitterness. What gives it its authority is the fact that it affirms the truth, shares with others the gifts of charity, is itself an example of virtue, avoids peremptory language, makes no demands. It is peaceful, has no use for extreme methods, is patient under contradiction and inclines towards generosity.

3) Confidence is also necessary — confidence not only in the power of one's own words, but also in the good will of both parties to the dialogue. Hence dialogue promotes intimacy and friendship on both sides. It unites them in a mutual adherence to the Good, and thus excludes all self-seeking.

4) Finally, the prudence of a teacher who is most careful to make allowances for the psychological and moral circumstances

of his hearer, (57) particularly if he is a child, unprepared, suspicious or hostile. The person who speaks is always at pains to learn the sensitivities of his audience, and if reason demands it, he adapts himself and the manner of his presentation to the susceptibilities and the degree of intelligence of his hearers.

82. In a dialogue conducted with this kind of foresight, truth is wedded to charity and understanding to love.

Deeper Knowledge Through Wider Exposure

83. And that is not all. For it becomes obvious in a dialogue that there are various ways of coming to the light of faith and it is possible to make them all converge on the same goal. However divergent these ways may be, they can often serve to complete each other. They encourage us to think on different lines. They force us to go more deeply into the subject of our investigations and to find better ways of expressing ourselves. It will be a slow process of thought, but it will result in the discovery of elements of truth in the opinion of others and make us want to express our teaching with great fairness. It will be set to our credit that we expound our doctrine in such a way that others can respond to it, if they will, and assimilate it gradually. It will make us wise; it will make us teachers.

Modes of Dialogue

84. Consider now the form the dialogue of salvation takes and the manner of exposition.

85. It has many forms. If necessary it takes account of actual experience. It chooses appropriate means. It is unencumbered by prejudice. It does not hold fast to forms of expression which have lost their meaning and can no longer stir men's minds.

Ecclesiam Suam, paragraphs 81-85.

Given at St. Peter's, Rome, on the Feast of the Transfiguration of Our Lord Jesus Christ, the sixth day of August, in the year 1964, the second of Our Pontificate.

Bridge Building in the Presbyterate: Spirituality as the Common Ground

Rev. Paul J. Philibert, OP

Some decades ago, a French periodical addressed the diversity of roles of post-Vatican II priests with the jaunty remark, "Remember, God doesn't spend all his time in church."[1] The church in France was coping with a decline in Sunday Mass attendance and the loss of the working class. Christian "presence" in society was the reigning pastoral solution. That included small communities, social action and intense efforts at youth work — especially through Young Christian Students and Young Christian Workers. The buzzword of the day was *"la pastorale d'ensernble,"* roughly translatable as "clergy-lay pastoral teams." Priests were being warned that their role was only one in a continuum of factors that fused together to enable the efficacy of the church in a diverse society.

In the U.S. just a few years later, the NCCB undertook a massive effort to study the priesthood in this country, commissioning sociological, psychological and historical studies that have become landmarks of empirical research on Catholic ministry. A part of this initiative was the production of the classic, *The Spiritual Renewal of the American Priesthood* (SRAP).[2] This brief book about the spirituality of American priests was the work of a team of competent, experienced priests and theologians whose individual contributions and group work were edited and written up by Carmelite Father Ernest Larkin. Published in 1973, SRAP set itself the goal of helping priests interpret and respond to the onslaught of new experiences arising out of the reforms of the council. Those challenges included negotiating the vernacular liturgy and the reconfigured sanctuary, integrating the council's new emphasis on the biblical word and on the homily, and managing the growth of role expectations for priests and the multiplication of ministries in parishes. SRAP's great contribution was its sustained analysis of the life and ministry of priests in the light of the Paschal Mystery of Jesus and the spirituality that flows from that.

A few years ago, the National Federation of Priests' Councils was alert to the impending thirtieth anniversary of SRAP. In 1998, Executive Director Bernard Stratman undertook to organize a concerted program that included colloquia, research initiatives and the commissioning of an anniversary document. This document's aim would be to assess the areas of change in the priesthood since 1973 and to revisit the goals for the spirituality of priests in these new circumstances. It is now published by Liturgical Press with the title *Stewards of God's Mysteries: Priestly Spirituality in a Changing Church*.[3] It is the work of a team that includes the well-known Diocese of Oakland pastor, Father Dan Danielson; Sulpician Father Mel Blanchette, the director of the Vatican II Institute in Menlo Park; and myself as writer.

Stewards was written with close attention to what NFPC had learned about priests during its colloquia on ministry, formation and spirituality. NFPC commissioned two studies from the respected religious sociologist Dean Hoge, which have now been published as *The First Five Years of Priesthood* and *Evolving Visions of the Priesthood*.[4] From these studies as well as from focus groups and conversations with more recently ordained priests, we learned that there is a new cohort of priests characterized by their distance from the Second Vatican Council and by their firm loyalty to Pope John Paul II. They share what might be described as a nostalgia for pre-Vatican II days (grounded not in their own experience but in the opinions of people they respect). Trying to effect mutual understanding between them and the older cohorts of priests and to build solidarity among them became the clear priority that emerged from our research. A continuing rift among U.S. priests about vision and strategies for pastoral effectiveness would become a wound from which the church might not easily recover.

The Issue of Laity in Ministry

Younger U.S. priests are not the only ones who imagine that the implementation of Vatican II has somehow been responsible for diminishing the status of priests. On November 13, 1997, at a Vatican press conference held for the release of the influential 1997 Instruction on the "Collaboration of Non-ordained Faithful in Priests' Sacred Ministry," Curial officials remarked as follows: "Lay ministries that obscure the differences between ordained priests and the laity, even if motivated by a desire to serve priestless communities, are harmful to the church."[5] On the same occasion, Archbishop Dario Castrillon Hoyos, pro-prefect of the Congregation for the Clergy, explained the purpose of the instruction by saying that it provides norms to overcome "the phenomenon of the clericalization of the laity and the secularization of the clergy."[6] To the ears of someone who was alive and had followed the developments of Vatican II in the 1960s, these statements at the Vatican press conference may sound like backtracking to a pre-conciliar vision of church. However, we must take great care to sort through the many dimensions of this issue. It is not a simple matter.

This question of the relation between ordained ministers of the church and non-ordained lay ecclesial ministers has become a magnet that attracts much of the energy and anxiety of troubled persons on both sides of the divide. We simply must get beyond the impasse created by older clergy dismissing their juniors as self-preoccupied traditionalists on the one hand, and the more recently ordained scorning senior clergy as liberal loose cannons on the other. Is there a way to do this? We think so.

Stewards consistently focuses on creating an agenda for dialogue that can bring bishops together with both their senior and their junior clergy to re-examine the fundamentals of the ministry and the spirituality of the ordained. Each chapter of *Stewards* concludes with a set of reflection questions for individual readers and another set for group study. These aids facilitate the kind of dialogue that will engage priests in partnerships rather than rivalries.

Solid Principles

The recent apostolic exhortation of Pope John Paul II, *Pastores Gregis*, summarizes many of the principles that are the foundation for the work we did with *Stewards*. Unfortunately, *Pastores Gregis* appeared a few months after our book had gone to press, or we would have drawn from it. I will cite one paragraph here, however, as a source for reflection on the key issues that are at the heart of *Stewards of God's Mysteries*. In paragraph 10, the Holy Father writes:

The interplay between the common priesthood of the faithful and the ministerial priesthood, present in the episcopal ministry itself, is manifested in a kind of *perichoresis* between the two forms of priesthood: a *perichoresis* between the common witness to the faith given by the faithful and the bishop's authoritative witness to the faith through his magisterial acts; a *perichoresis* between the lived holiness of the faithful and the means of sanctification that the bishop offers them; and finally, a *perichoresis* between the personal responsibility of the bishop for the good of the church entrusted to him and the shared responsibility of all the faithful for that same church.[7]

This Greek term *perichoresis*, used in the English translation of *Pastores Gregis* (the Latin official text has *motus circularis*), comes from Trinitarian theology and describes the ongoing mutual interchange of life and energy among equals. This is not the place to exegete the apostolic exhortation; it is much too rich to reduce its teaching to this single paragraph. However, it is very much to the point to note the mutuality and reciprocity in the interplay between baptismal priesthood and ministerial priesthood described here.

Stewards undertakes to elucidate the very relationships described in *Pastores Gregis*, namely, quality preaching by the ordained and apostolic witness by the faithful; spiritual depth in the ordained and the sanctification of the families and work of the faithful; and pastoral leadership for the common good of the community and genuine collaboration engaging the competencies and passion of the faithful. These are the very issues whose productive resolution will shape the future well-being of the American Church.

Focal Issues

Returning to the question of what shaped the agenda of *Stewards*, we found three areas where some significant shift of emphasis has taken place in ordained ministry since 1973. Naturally, all three of these areas of concern were recognized and mentioned in SRAP. However, the 30 ensuing years have been a period in which considerable evolution has occurred on these points. Therefore the attention that *Stewards* devotes to them is different in perspective and in depth.

First, priestly ministry can be described as having moved from a *cultic* to a *comprehensive* model. The documents of Vatican II, especially *Lumen Gentium* (LG) and *Presbyterorum Ordinis* (PO), provided the necessary clues to this evolution. PO §4 calls preaching, the proclamation of God's saving word, the "first task of priests as co-workers of the bishops." LG §10 and PC §2 establish the principle that the ministerial priesthood exists precisely to enable and serve the common priesthood of the baptized.[8] In *Pastores Gregis* §10, Pope John Paul speaks of the ministry of the bishop as "being for" the other members of the faithful, even as the bishop continues "being with" them in the common priesthood.

These themes, now central to the church's self-understanding, are dynamic points of departure for the theological reflection in *Stewards*. The baptismal (common) priesthood is the object of the church's ministerial service, and the mission of the church is achieved in the fundamental collaboration of the two priesthoods. The implications of this teaching have led to a keener appreciation of the multi-faceted profile of the ministry of priests.

In *Stewards*, following what we learned from research and experience, we describe six roles exercised by the ordained, calling them: 1) vicar of the bishop, 2) bearer of the mystery (mystagogue), 3) spiritual personality, 4) pastoral leader, 5) model of human authenticity and 6) prophet. Each of these is explained in detail, drawing upon both magisterial teaching and the experience of pastors in today's church. The explanation of these six roles is a concrete way of describing the comprehensive nature of priestly ministry today. We are counting on earnest dialogue across diverse generations and pastoral experience to flesh out and develop the significance of this exploration of a "comprehensive" model of priestly ministry. A firm common understanding of this profile of roles is critical to presbyterates' effectiveness and to their capacity for mutual moral support.

A second area where matters have changed, more in degree than in kind, is the sphere of ministerial collaboration. Two-thirds of U.S. parishes now employ one or more (possibly several more) lay ecclesial ministers. The shift for the priest is from *control* to *collaboration*. In a fully functioning parish, there are now many areas where the execution of some part of the parish's mission is in the hands of lay helpers. Many of these elements are increasingly critical for building a living faith community.

For example, the effectiveness of lectors impacts powerfully upon the religious experience of the Sunday assembly. There are times when the lectionary readings, proclaimed with understanding, passion and faith, become justly the highlight of the Mass. Further, the role of those who offer hospitality and are on the lookout to welcome strangers and help them feel at home is likewise important. We hardly know yet how to shape this ministry of hospitality, so new is the idea, but for many seekers it will play a decisive factor in their returning to the parish or not.

The role of music ministers, especially when their preparations for the Sunday liturgies are integrated with the planning of the preacher/presider and other liturgical ministers, is very formative of a parish's worship life. The pastor depends upon their formation, their skills, and their generosity to assure requisite beauty and vitality to the parish's Sunday celebrations. A living celebration of a people of faith, rather than a materially correct performance of the rite of the Mass by the priest, will depend on a broad spectrum of well-prepared pastoral agents working in close cooperation.

In all of these cases, the priest operates in the delicate area of being the responsible overseer of these ministries on the one hand, and being respectful of the competencies, gifts and generosity of his assistants on the other hand. Many priests find oversight of the parish's ministries easier and more effective when exercised in the context of a pastoral team. Doing this well requires skills that arise from experience and learning. *Stewards* tries to help priests integrate this difficult area of their professional growth with their own spiritual development. In doing so, it offers resources to help them make the important transition from control to collaboration.

A third area of concentration for *Stewards* is the passage from *spiritual identity* to *spiritual practices*. All the talk in the world about spirituality is not going to effectively alter the way a priest lives his daily life. In tune with changes in retreat programs and in a recent writing on spiritual theology, *Stewards* looks very concretely at practices of daily prayer, retreats, spiritual direction, group study, and the integration of preaching preparation as formative for the spiritual life. Like Pope John Paul II's apostolic exhortation "I Will Give You Shepherds" following the Synod of Bishops on priestly ministry, *Stewards* expresses a real concern for the well-being of persons attempting to live this terribly demanding life of a Catholic priest.

> *The pressures of these times are terrific. Expectations for pastoral service have multiplied. Friction from complex relationships in collaborative ministry is inevitable. The wounding of the priest's public image from the recent publicizing of clerical sex abuse has been deflating and humiliating. The risk of exhaustion and burnout is genuine. In such a world, spiritual practices are a protection against depression and meltdown as well as the path of discipleship. Here again, we anticipate that the payoff in this area will come not just from reading what we have written, but also from frank sharing with the bishop and other priests in the light of what we have written.*

The burdens mentioned above are aggravated by feelings of disappointment or even betrayal with reference to other priests whose vision of church and ministry appears discordant with what we may consider the ideal. This, too, can be disheartening and draining. But this is a matter that can be remedied.

Even after reviewing the extensive research done by Dean Hoge and his associates, reading verbatims of focus groups and listening to the articulated frustrations of a great many priests, we still believe that what unites priests across generational and ideological differences is far stronger and more important than what divides them. It will require courageous initiatives on the part of bishops and real magnanimity on the part of priests to bring about the study/dialogue sessions that *Stewards* has been designed to create. But the stakes are high. What is at issue is the graceful movement of the U.S. church beyond the threshold of shame and exhaustion into a new springtime of energy and zeal.

These are issues that seminarians should be reflecting upon as well. *Stewards* will become, we hope, a resource for pastoral formation in Catholic seminaries and schools of theology. In those contexts, it would probably be advisable to introduce the voices of both senior and junior clergy from the diocese into the seminarians' discussions of *Stewards*. The book's discussion process is designed to move past fixed ideas and enter into honest exchange about pastoral experiences.

Perhaps I should conclude on this note of experience. Pastoral experience is before all else an experience of the anointing of the Holy Spirit. Priests have been anointed by the Spirit sacramentally in their baptism and confirmation as well as in their rite of ordination. But they are also anointed personally and experientially in the generous gift of themselves to their ministry. All the resources of their life become transfigured by the Spirit's action. For someone genuinely called and empowered to priestly service, the life is an amazement of grace and privilege.

To forgive in the name of God, to bless in the name of the risen Lord, to convoke the body of Christ in the name of the Holy Spirit — these are moments worth our whole selves. To give courage to the fearful, to reconcile the estranged, to fight for justice for the weak and powerless — these are inconceivable hopes, but for the love of God empowering us. The life of the Catholic priest is a living icon of the Paschal Mystery of Jesus. It is both the hardest thing and the most rewarding thing a person can do. As men called to be "stewards of God's mysteries" (1 Cor 4:1), priests are both privileged and vulnerable. I hope that the book called *Stewards* can help these privileged, vulnerable men accept their lives with deeper freedom and enjoy their ministry with greater delight. Above all, I hope that the common commitment of all these priests to the obedience of faith will unite them in a new solidarity for mission and renewal.

Paul J. Philibert, OP, is Distinguished Visiting Professor of Church and Society at Aquinas Institute of Theology in St. Louis, Missouri. During the 2003-04 academic year, he was theologian in residence at Mepkin Abbey in Moncks Corner, South Carolina.

END NOTES

1. Albert Bastenier, "Le Prêtre: chef d'orchestre ou témoin de Ia foi?," *La revue nouvelle* (15 Juin 1968) 625.

2. *The Spiritual Renewal of the American Priesthood* (Washington, D.C.: U.S.C.C., 1973).

3. Paul Philibert, *Stewards of God's Mysteries: Priestly Spirituality in a Changing Church* (Collegeville, Minn.: The Liturgical Press, 2004).

4. Dean R. Hoge, *The First Five Years of the Priesthood: A Study of Newly Ordained Catholic Priests* (Collegeville, Minn.: The Liturgical Press, 2002); and Dean R. Hoge and Jacqueline E. Wenger, *Evolving Visions of the Priesthood: Changes from Vatican II to the Turn of the New Century* (Collegeville, Minn.: The Liturgical Press, 2003).

5. Eight Vatican Offices, "Some Questions Regarding Collaboration of Nonordained Faithful in Priests' Sacred Ministry," *Origins* 27:24 (Nov. 27, 1997) 402/sidebar.

6. Ibid.

7. John Paul II, "Apostolic Exhortation Pastores Gregis," *Origins* 33:22 (Nov. 6, 2003) 360.

8. The Catechism of the Catholic Church expresses this relationship in these words: "While the common priesthood of the faithful is exercised by the unfolding of baptismal grace—a life of faith, hope, and charity, a life according to the Spirit—, the ministerial priesthood is at the service of the common priesthood. It is directed at the unfolding of the baptismal grace of all Christians." §1547.

Reprinted with permission from the NCEA Seminary Department. This article first appeared in Seminary Journal, *Volume 10, No.1 (Spring 2004).*

CHAPTER 3

SOME TOOLS FOR UNITY

Creating a Plan and Putting It Into Action

The crisis consists precisely in the fact that the old is dying and the new cannot be born. In this interregnum, a great variety of morbid symptoms appear.
Antonio Gramsci, political activist

It is one thing to diagnose a problem; it is another to know what to do to resolve it. Even if we do want an intentional presbyterate and even if we have leaders willing to work toward that dream, how to do it is still left for consideration. Here I am reminded of an old story I read years ago.

A certain weasel, long afflicted with neurotic symptoms, was accustomed to regular consultation with his psychiatrist, a wise old owl. As therapy progressed, the weasel, becoming disaffected with the long probing, the attempt to achieve insight into unconscious motivation and the wearisome effort to release emotional tensions, demanded of the owl, "Tell me what I should do!"

Taken aback both by the unexpected nature and by the vehemence of the demand, the owl abandoned his customary reserve and ventured direct advice. "I think, my dear weasel," he said at last, "that the only solution to your problem is to turn yourself into a frog."

The weasel was astonished at this advice and replied, "Thank you for your advice, which I fully tend to heed. One problem remains, however. I pray, sir, tell me how I go about turning myself into a frog."

To this the owl replied, with a certain measure of disdain, "My dear weasel, please be kind enough not to bother me with these operational problems."[42]

1. A Priestly Life and Ministry Cluster

If we are to have intentional presbyterates, the place to begin, it would seem to me, is to look at how we are organized now. In many dioceses, including my own, there are several offices that deal with the ministry and lives of priests, but they do not formally collaborate. While most offices are doing a decent job, there is no regular dialogue among them. It seems to me that if the goal is to have a unified presbyterate, the place to begin would be to create some kind of "priestly life and ministry cluster" so the left hand will know what the right hand is doing. Regular collaboration should take place among the vocation office, the priest personnel office, the continuing education office, the priests' health panel and the office of retired priests. This cluster, coming together for regular collaboration, could help focus our common wisdom toward strengthening us individually and as a group.

The first goal of such a cluster would be to look at everything that is already available to support priests (as a group and individually), to identify what is missing, and to put it all back together in a comprehensive and intentional plan for ongoing presbyteral health and effectiveness.

2. What Help is Currently Available?

Many priests under-use, or may even be ignorant of, the help that is already available to them. Most dioceses have all or some of the following supports.

- The laity
- The bishop
- Fellow priests
- Family and friends
- Financial compensation
- Office of clergy personnel
- Continuing formation of the clergy office
- Clergy health panel
- Priests' council
- Vicar for clergy
- Retired housing

- Presbyteral assembly
- Support groups
- Annual retreats, prayer days and prayer groups
- Sabbaticals
- Spiritual directors
- Alternative housing
- Vacations
- Chrism Mass
- Clergy Day
- Priests' Jubilee celebration
- Ordination celebrations

3. Doing Group Maintenance: The Role of the Presbyteral Assembly

A "priestly life and ministry cluster" could be the nucleus of a team created to refocus attention on the continued health and effectiveness not only of individual members of a presbyterate, but also of the presbyterate as a team. For continued health and effectiveness, every organization needs to tend to "task maintenance" (getting the job done well) and "group maintenance" (taking good care of those who do the job). "Task maintenance" tends to the *effectiveness* of those who do ministry. "Group maintenance" tends to the *health and cohesiveness* of those who do ministry. Continuing education offices deal primarily with the *effectiveness* of ministry. Groups like the health panel take care of individual priests who do the ministry. The premier event that deals with the health and cohesiveness of the group, the event that could focus most effectively on forming intentional presbyterates, I believe, is the annual Presbyteral Assembly. For this reason, the planning of this annual assembly should be a major concern of the "priestly life and ministry cluster" since they have, together, the big picture of what is going on in our presbyterates.

An important part of doing "group maintenance" is mentoring new members into the presbyterate. This will necessitate the need to include seminarians in as many presbyteral functions as possible (and to schedule them so that they can). Seminarians need to know not only how to be a good seminarian, but also how to be a good priest. Even though some would like to look at the recruitment and training of seminarians as separate from the issues facing presbyterates, I do not share that view. I fought against this "not in front of the kids" mentality throughout my time as a vocation director. Some believe that since seminarians are not yet priests, they should be treated as something radically different until after their ordinations. I do not accept this view any more than I accept the view that a fetus is not a baby until it is actually born or that prenatal care has nothing to do with the later health of that child. Even wolves wait together at the lair for the birth of a cub and, once born, the whole pack takes responsibility for, and participates in, training them to work as a team and to be contributing members of their pack.

As Pope John Paul II said in "I Will Give You Shepherds," the bishop can rely above all on the cooperation of his presbyterate (in promoting vocations). All its priests are united to the bishop and share his responsibility in seeking and fostering vocations."[43]

The facts are that more than 25% of all new priests now are "foreign born," and many others are "converts." As a group, their seminary training has been dramatically shortened compared with that of priests in the past. While these "outsiders" have the chance of working with three or four pastors during summer assignments, it is usually not possible for them to meet most of the presbyterate until after their ordinations. It is simply too dangerous to continue this practice of introducing new priests to their presbyterates on their ordination days and putting the burden on them to find their own way in bonding with the group. Paul de Becker, in a recent article in *The Tablet* titled "A Priest Alone," says of the newly ordained who struggle in ministry: "A root cause of their unhappiness and a major element in their lives is an intense loneliness."[44]

It is insane to warn a new priest not to become a "lone ranger" and then not give him an alternative. As Bishop Gerald Kicanas, a former seminary rector and now a bishop, has said, "The call to priesthood would be responded to more freely if the fear of intense loneliness were not as prominent."[45]

Including and involving seminarians in presbyteral assemblies, from the beginning, gives them a chance to get to know most priests before ordination. Such an involvement gives most priests an opportunity to support those in training and tell them how much we value their sacrifices, even if their parish has no seminarians or has not had the chance to welcome one of them for a summer placement. Priests-to-be need to see us and hear from us, and we need to see them and hear from them as well. All the recent research tells us that contact with priests is still the best way to promote and keep vocations to the priesthood. When that is not done, most other efforts fail.

A lot has been said about making attendance at presbyteral assemblies "mandatory." While I believe that the bishop has the right to demand participation for the sake of the group, I believe the better path is for those who plan these assemblies to make them so attractive that most will want to attend. Force is useless. Let it be a coalition of the "willing," not of the "coerced."

4. A "Pastors in Training" Program

Besides the "group mentoring into the presbyterate by the whole presbyterate" that should begin as soon as a seminarian is accepted by the diocese (see section 3), there is a serious need for individual mentors for the newly ordained, leading up to and including a first pastorate.

Problem: In recent years, the newly ordained and new pastors have been assigned a priest mentor, usually a model pastor. The results have been mixed. One of the main problems being reported is the failure to meet regularly. A fine pastor may not have the time necessary for this work. A model pastor may not know how to teach what he knows.

Possible Solution: Choose a small group of our best retired priests, maybe three who are willing to serve as "group mentors" for new pastors. Do some initial formation and training of that group, and choose a leader.

Problem: The newly ordained are being named pastors in a year or two. Seminary did not and cannot prepare them to be pastors. Associate pastors are reporting that they are neither fish nor fowl, with no real position in many parish structures. A week-long or weekend orientation for being a pastor is not adequate.

Solution: Once a new priest is ordained, he could be called a "pastor in formation" while serving as an "associate pastor" at a designated parish. Because no single small diocese would have enough "new pastors" for their own program, a new inter-diocesan "pastors in formation" program could be mapped out by the continuing education directors of neighboring dioceses. Because it is "inter-diocesan," various types of groups could formed around the various types of parishes they will be going into: urban parishes, rural parishes, home mission parishes, clustered parishes, ethnic parishes. A qualified leader for the group should be selected and trained, if necessary. Because of all its resources, this leader and this group of new pastors-to-be could hold their quarterly meetings at the "regional center for sustaining pastoral excellence" (see section 5). Problems and situations are presented and worked through by the group. Exceptional pastors, lay ministry leaders and other professionals would be asked to be presenters in this program. Anyone who hopes to become a pastor should meet the basic requirements of this program. An evaluation of their participation and learning is presented to the bishop and personnel committee for consideration in an assignment as pastor.

Problem: Many times entry-into-new-pastorate-problems are not addressed as they happen, but are left to fester. Often only the priest is asked about how things are going. Asking the new pastor to self-report his problems is an unreal expectation.

Solution: Once the new pastor has been named, the group mentors should meet with his parish council before he begins; with the new pastor, his staff and parish council six months into the process; and again six months after that until it has been established that it is no longer necessary. Regular reports are made to the bishop until he is no longer considered a "new pastor."

5. Regional Centers For Sustaining Pastoral Excellence

Seminary is not enough! I learned that as soon as I was ordained. Like all my classmates, I was trained to be an associate pastor in a large suburban parish or small city parish. I was expected to learn to be a pastor on the job over a ten- to twelve-year period. However,

I was sent to our "home missions." It was unusual in 1975, but I ended up being a pastor after five years. I was not prepared to start a new parish, to live alone or to understand the dynamics of the "bible belt." I had to learn on the job. Cut off from most other priests, I had to teach myself. Neither was I prepared to handle the rural parish and an old cathedral in need of revitalization that followed my first assignment. I was left to figure out what to do on my own.

In 2003, we are still ordaining good men and sending them into ministry situations that they are not prepared to handle, with shallow and haphazard support systems and disconnected ongoing education programs. When these young pastors crash and burn, we seem surprised and, in many cases, blame the victim or the seminary that trained them. This is exacerbated by the fact that young priests are now being given large parishes within a year or two after ordination, and many of those young priests are foreign born or recent "converts."

Most American seminaries are doing a heroic job at what they do, but there is no way they can accomplish everything that is needed while these young men are in the seminary. All that seminaries can realistically offer, under their present configuration, is a sound theological base and a taste of pastoral ministry. They cannot do all that is necessary to prepare serious pastoral leaders before ordination.

What we need, I believe, are "regional centers for sustaining pastoral excellence" designed to support priests in ministry. These regional centers should be just as serious in their approach as our seminaries are at preparing priests to enter ministry. Since Vatican II, we have put all our eggs in the workshop-convention model of continuing education. That model is increasingly inadequate. What we need is something organized, intentional, structured, lifelong and, in some cases, mandatory. This kind of program must be focused not so much on academics, but on helping priests to do their work well by staying healthy, engaged and prepared to meet the new challenges they face, whether they be in a first pastorate or a rural, missionary, inner-city or multicultural parish or ministry situation.

This kind of serious, well-thought-out approach to the practice of ministry needs, in most cases, to be accomplished across diocesan lines. Very few dioceses have the resources and skilled personnel to adequately teach these skills. A serious collaboration among the continuing formation directors of neighboring dioceses could lead to the foundation of such an enterprise. As far as money, most priests do not use the continuing education funds already available to them.

With some renovation and expansion, already existing seminary sites would be ideal. They already have theological libraries, bookstores, spiritual directors, confessors, chapels, liturgies, housing, an established communication network, gyms and retreat-like atmospheres. These "regional centers for sustaining pastoral excellence," sharing the same campus with seminarians, could complete a seminary's mission of providing well-trained diocesan priests for its client dioceses. Having these centers on the campus of, but separate from, the seminary could raise the theological level of priests, while providing an on-site laboratory for seminarians to observe real pastoral ministers in dialogue and problem solving. Add ongoing deacon and lay ministry formation, and the picture is even more complete.

As a vocation director, I was not only interested in attracting more vocations to priesthood, but also in keeping the vocations we have happy, healthy and effective. In that job, I tried to train our seminarians to "mind their calls" after ordination, but I am only one person. All priests share in the duty. We need to give each other that challenge, but we also need to give each other the structures to do it.

Some Major Insights on Priests and Presbyterates from Church Documents

Christus Dominus

#28

All priests, both diocesan and religious, participate in and exercise with the bishop the one priesthood of Christ and are thereby meant to be prudent cooperators of the Episcopal order ... pastoring a single portion of the Lord's flock.

In order to distribute the sacred ministries more equitably and properly among his priests, the bishop should posses a necessary freedom in assigning offices and benefices. Therefore, the right or privileges, which in any way limit this freedom, are to be suppressed.

The harmony of the will of the priests with that of the bishop will render their pastoral activity more fruitful ... thereby (helping priests) develop a pressing concern for the spiritual welfare of the whole diocese.

Presbyterorum Ordinis

#7

No priest can in isolation or single handedly accomplish his mission in a satisfactory way. He can do so only by joining forces with other priests under the direction of Church authorities.

#7, Footnote 87

In stating that priests are "necessary helpers and counselors," the Decree wants to make clear that such priestly help and counsel are not a kind of intrinsic luxury at the whim of the bishop to use or not, nor can this priestly help and counsel be substituted by any other.

#8

All priests are united among themselves in an intimate sacramental brotherhood. In a special way they form one presbytery in a diocese to whose service they are committed under their own bishop.

Optatam Totius

#2

Let (each priest) attract the hearts of young people to the priesthood by his own humble and energetic life, joyfully pursued, and by love for his fellow priests and brotherly collaboration with them.

Pastores Dabo Vobis

#17

Ordained ministry has a radical communitarian form and can only be carried out as collective work.

The ministry of priests is above all communion with the bishop's ministry, in concern for the universal Church and for the individual particular churches, for whose service they form with the bishop a single presbyterate.

The ministerial priesthood and the common priesthood of the faithful, which differ essentially and not only in degree, are ordered one to another – for each in its own way derives from the one priesthood of Christ.

The ministerial priesthood does not of itself signify a greater degree of holiness with regard to the common priesthood of the faithful.

Christ gives to priests, in the Spirit, a particular gift so that they can help the People of God to exercise faithfully and fully the common priesthood, which it has received.

#18

Because the priest is a man of communion, in his relations with all people he must be a man of mission and dialogue.

#21

The spiritual life of the ministers of the New Testament should be marked by a fundamental attitude of service to the People of God, freed from all presumption or desire of "lording it over" those in their charge.

#23

Within the Church community the priest's pastoral charity impels and demands in particular and specific ways his personal relationship with the presbyterate, united in and with the bishop.

#26

The priest is first of all a minister of the word of God. For this reason, the priest himself ought to develop a great personal familiarity with the word of God. Only if he "abides" in the word will the priest become a perfect disciple of the Lord. The priest ought to be the first "believer" in the word, while being fully aware that the words of his ministry are not "his," but those of the One who sent him. Precisely because he can and does evangelize, the priest ought to grow in awareness that he himself is continually in need of being evangelized. In order that he is transmitting the Gospel in its fullness, the priest is called to develop a special sensitivity, love and docility to the living tradition of the Church and her *magisterium*, which serve its proper interpretation and preserve its authentic meaning.

It is above all in the celebration of the sacraments and in the celebration of the Liturgy of the Hours that the priest is called to live and witness to the deep unity between the exercise of the ministry and his spiritual life. From the various sacraments the priest's spiritual life is built up and molded by the different characteristics and demands of each of the sacraments as he celebrates and experiences them.

A priest is called to express in his life the authority and service of Christ by gathering together and leading the Church. This involves the ability to coordinate all the gifts and charisms in the community, to discern them and to put them to good use for the upbuilding of the Church in constant union with the bishops. This ministry demands of the priest an intense spiritual life, filled with those qualities and virtues typical of a person who "presides over" and "leads" a community.

#28

Among the virtues most necessary for the priestly ministry must be named that disposition by which priests are always ready to seek not their own will, but the will of him who sent them.

Obedience is first of all "apostolic" in the sense that it recognizes, loves and serves the Church in her hierarchical structure because there can be no genuine priestly ministry except in communion with the supreme pontiff and the Episcopal college, especially with one's own diocesan bishop to whom the priest promised "filial respect and obedience" during the rite of ordination.

Only the person who knows how to obey in Christ is really able to require obedience from others in his ministry.

Priestly obedience has a "community dimension." It is not the obedience of an individual who alone relates to authority, but rather an obedience that is deeply a part of the unity of the presbyterate.

Priestly obedience demands a marked spirit of asceticism in the sense of not being too bound up in one's own preferences or points of view.

Priestly obedience demands a marked spirit of asceticism in the sense of giving brother priests the opportunity to make good use of their talents and abilities, setting aside all forms of jealousy, envy and rivalry.

Priestly obedience should be one of solidarity, based on belonging to a single presbyterate. Within the presbyterate, this obedience is expressed in co-responsibility regarding direction to be taken and choices to be made.

Priestly obedience has a particular "pastoral" character when it is lived in an atmosphere of constant readiness to allow oneself to be taken up, as it were "consumed," by the needs and demands of the flock.

#29

Celibacy is a precious gift given by God to his Church as a sign of the kingdom, which is not of this world — a sign of God's love for this world and of an undivided love of the priest for God and for God's people. It is especially important that the priest understand the theological motivation of the Church's law on celibacy. In as much as it is a law, it expresses the Church's will, even before the will of the subject expressed his readiness.

#31

All (priests) are required to make a sincere effort to live in mutual esteem, to respect others, and to hold in esteem all the positive and legitimate diversities present in the presbyterate. This, too, constitutes part of the priest's spiritual life and his continual practice of asceticism.

#43

Of special importance is the capacity (of the priest) to relate to others. This is truly fundamental for a person who is called to be a "man of communion." This demands that a priest not be arrogant or quarrelsome, but affable, hospitable, sincere in his words and heart, prudent and discreet, generous and ready to serve, capable of opening himself to clear and brotherly relationships and of encouraging the same in others, and quick to understand, forgive and console.

#69

All formation, priestly formation included, is ultimately a self-formation.

#70

Ongoing formation is an intrinsic requirement of the gift and sacramental ministry received; and it proves necessary in every age. It is particularly urgent today because of rapid changes in the social and cultural conditions of individuals and people among whom priestly ministry is exercised.

#74

The priest is called in particular to grow, thanks to his ongoing formation, in and with his own presbyterate in union with the bishop.

Unity among priests with the bishop and among themselves is not something added from the outside to the nature of their service, but expresses its essence inasmuch as it ... makes priests witnesses of Jesus Christ, who prayed "that they may all be one."

Priestly unity excludes no one. This fraternity takes special care of the young priests, maintains a kind and fraternal dialogue with those of the middle and older age groups and with those who for whatever reasons are facing difficulties; as for those priests who have given up this way of life or are not following it at this time, this brotherhood does not forget them but follows them all the more with fraternal solicitude.

This fraternity maintains a kind and fraternal dialogue...with those who for whatever reasons are facing difficulties. As for those priests who have given up this way of life or are not following it at this time, this brotherhood does not forget them but follows them all the more with fraternal solicitude.

Religious clergy who live and work in a particular church also belong to the one presbyterate. Their presence is a source of enrichment for all priests. For their part, religious will be concerned to ensure a spirit of true ecclesial communion, a genuine participation in the progress of the diocese and the pastoral decisions of the bishop, generously putting their own charism at the service of building up everyone in charity.

#79

In a certain sense, it is the priest himself, the individual priest, who is the person primarily responsible in the Church for his ongoing formation.

THE BASIC PLAN FOR THE ONGOING FORMATION OF PRIESTS PART III

USCCB

Priests are not priests simply one by one, but they are priests and serve the mission of the church in a presbyterate with the bishop.

Divisions in presbyterates lead to diminished effectiveness, undermine the resources needed to address pressing problems, constitute an anti-sign for the community of the faith, discourage those who might feel called to the priesthood and shift the focus from a wide-ranging diocesan perspective to parochialism and congregationalism.

To pursue the ongoing formation not simply of (individual) priests, but of a presbyterate as a whole, brings us to new territory. The corporate sense of priestly identity and mission, although not fully developed even in official documents, is clearly emerging as an important direction for the future.

Far from being closed in on itself, a truly unified presbyterate dynamically redirects itself outward in pastoral charity. The formation of a presbyterate in its unity and fraternity aims, ultimately, to promote a more intense pastoral charity … and makes it a more transparent sacramental sign … of God's plan of unity for the Church and for all humanity.

The formation of the presbyterate in its unity is the responsibility of all its members.

The fraternal bonds of a presbyterate are forged and deepened not only in the context of prayer and work done together but also through the informal contact that priests in a presbyterate have with one another. These become occasions of mutual recognition and support and, on occasion, of healthy challenge. Given the pace of parish life and time demands that are made on priests, a kind of planned spontaneity may be the only way that such informal contact can be made.

The examination of divisions in presbyterates leads to a practical conclusion about the necessity of deliberately linking priests across different categories. It is important to link priests across generational lines, theological persuasions, ethnicity and differences in places of origin. It will not happen spontaneously. It needs explicit commitment on the part of the priests and some creative and deliberate mechanisms of implementation.

CANON LAW

#245.2

Seminary students are to be so formed that they are prepared for fraternal union with the diocesan presbyterate whose partners they will be in service of the Church.

#529.2

A pastor is to cooperate with his own bishop and the presbyterate of the diocese, also working so that the faithful have a concern for parochial communion, consider themselves members of the diocese and of the universal Church, and participate in and sustain efforts to promote this same communion.

Intentional Presbyterates I-A
Claiming Our Common Sense of Purpose as Diocesan Priests
A Presbyteral Assembly Model

The following presbyteral assembly model is provided by the Institute for Priests and Presbyterates, a program of Saint Meinrad Seminary and School of Theology, to help create an event that will serve the needs of the presbyterate and be based on the teachings of the Church. The conferences listed in this assembly model are provided by Fr. J. Ronald Knott, Director of the Institute for Priests and Presbyterates, and are designed to be given by selected priests and lay people of your diocese.

In addition to this particular presbyteral assembly model, a retreat model has also been created and is included in this book.

"Claiming Our Common Sense of Purpose as Diocesan Priests" is the first of four themes designed for building presbyteral unity.

Intentional Presbyterates II: "Honoring the Variety of Gifts within our Presbyterate" focuses on how giving fellow priests opportunities to share their gifts and talents with one another is part of the work of building presbyteral unity and constitutes part of a priest's spiritual life.

Intentional Presbyterates III: "Made Holy by Our Shared Ministry" is based on themes from *Pastores Dabo Vobis*, concentrating on how a priest's three-fold ministry is his principal means of sanctification.

Intentional Presbyterates IV: "The Asceticism of Dialogue in the Ministry of Unity" is based on a theme within Pope Paul VI's encyclical *Ecclesiam Suam* to help priests learn to speak with one another more effectively.

For more detailed instructions on hosting Intentional Presbyterates I-A, Presbyteral Assembly Model, purchase the Intentional Presbyterates Workbook at Saint Meinrad's Scholar Shop or online at http://store.saintmeinrad.edu.

> *"Stir into flame the gift of God that you have through the imposition of my hands"*
> 2 Timothy 1:6

GOALS

A. To move to a consensus on a new vision for our presbyterate built on the old;

B. To invite our presbyterate to commit to that new vision;

C. To find new ways to keep that new vision before our eyes and to pass it on to new members, and

D. To involve some of the lay and religious talent of the diocese to help strengthen our presbyteral unity.

INPUT SECTION

WHERE ARE WE?

THE HISTORY, CHARISM AND SPIRITUALITY OF DIOCESAN PRESBYTERATES

The opening speaker places the assembly topic in context by addressing some of the following questions: What are presbyterates? What does the church say about presbyterates and their relationships to diocesan bishops? How do religious priests working in a diocese fit into local presbyterates? What is specific to the spirituality of diocesan priests?

A HISTORICAL OVERVIEW OF THE LOCAL PRESBYTERATE

This speaker, a respected local historian, will be encouraged to write a short history of the local presbyterate in particular, not just a history of the diocese in general. This speaker identifies the great personalities, significant events and other major forces, like immigration, that have shaped the local presbyterate since the beginning.

The Local Presbyterate as We Have Known It

This speaker, an articulate older priest, will give a reflection on the presbyterate he and his contemporaries have known. It is expected that he will interview other older priests and gather their insights as part of his reflections. His emphasis should be objective and free of blame and personal complaints.

The Local Presbyterate as We Hope to Experience It

An articulate younger priest will summarize the hopes and fears of the young members of the local presbyterate. Again, it is expected that the speaker will summarize his conversations with other newly ordained and older seminarians. Again, his emphasis should be objective and free of blame and personal complaints. It is suggested that seminarians in Theology attend and participate, not only in this assembly, but other major priest gatherings, since this is called for by Canon 245:2.

What it is Like to Enter Our Presbyterate as an Outsider

An articulate international priest, a newly incardinated priest and a religious priest will summarize the experiences of those new to the presbyterate, spelling out what worked and what would have worked better in the welcoming process.

What Lay People are Looking for From Their Priests

An articulate layman and laywoman summarize the expectations of priests by the laity: what they have liked and what they would like to see. This presentation is expected to be both positive and challenging.

A Vision of Bishop and Priests Working Together: A Bishop's Perspective

The bishop gives his vision for how he and the priests can function united with one another.

WHAT HELP DO WE PRESENTLY HAVE? A Report

In this talk, the Vicar for Priests, the Director of Ongoing Formation or some other priest reviews the programs, celebrations and services currently available to priests individually and as a presbyterate.

Process Section

WHERE DO WE WANT TO GO FROM HERE?

This section requires a person with remarkable process skills. His task will be to get a consensus on some basic responsibilities individual priests owe the group and on some basic responsibilities the group owes to individual priests.

What are our individual responsibilities to the presbyterate, and what are the responsibilities of the presbyterate to us as individuals?

What additional help do priests need, individually and as a presbyterate?

A review of all annual presbyteral celebrations: What works and what does not? What would work better?

To what are we willing to commit?

Celebration Section

- Banquet Honoring Those Who Have Anniversaries (optional)
- Prayer Service
- Recreational Opportunities, Entertainment and Food
- Closing Eucharist and Ritual Re-Commitment

Follow-Up Section

Keeping the Vision Before Our Eyes

A writing committee will summarize the proceedings, putting them in a useful written form for distribution and review.

A "Priestly Life and Ministry Cluster" (representatives from various diocesan offices serving priests) will make plans on how to keep the vision before our eyes, build on it, and plan follow-up assemblies, retreats and celebrations.

Sharing the Vision

Getting the word out will be accomplished by:

- Collaborating with the diocesan communications office on how to share this process and its vision with the people of the diocese

- Publishing all documents for homebound priests, seminarians and other future new presbyteral members.

Additional Things to Consider

- According to Canon 245.2, "seminarians, while they are in the seminary, are to be trained to take their places in the diocesan presbyterate." Inviting them to attend could be a wonderful opportunity for "group mentoring."

- The main reason for a unified presbyterate is to offer better quality pastoral ministry to the People of God. Having this event covered in the diocesan paper, with pictures, could be an opportunity to educate the laity on the presbyterate's efforts of ongoing formation.

- Involving the laity in an evening music concert and dessert event would give them a chance to show their appreciation for the ministry of priests in a non-intrusive way.

- Because dioceses and presbyterates are different, creative additions or subtractions to this outline are encouraged.

- Planning committee questions can be addressed to Fr. Ronald Knott at rknott@saintmeinrad.edu.

- If this model is used, a donation to the Saint Meinrad Institute for Priests and Presbyterates would be most welcome.

FEEDBACK FROM THOSE WHO HAVE USED THIS ASSEMBLY MODEL

On behalf of our continuing formation director I would like to thank you for the fine presentation you gave at our Priest Convocation. So many priests were grateful for your timely words. One priest commented, "(the speaker) hit all the nails on the head." May God continue to bless you and your ministry! Thank you for the generous gift of yourself, especially for the priests of the United States.
Most Reverend R. Walter Nickless, Bishop of Sioux City

I have been a priest for 46 years, and as I participated in your workshop, I realized more than ever the great need that I, as the Bishop of the Diocese, have for an "Intentional Presbyterate." Also, in thinking back over my past many years as a priest, I believe that this goal should have been set for every presbyterate a long time ago. I would certainly recommend this workshop to any Diocese and any brother Bishop.
Most Reverend John J. McRaith, Bishop of Owensboro

I wanted to thank you for the recent presentations. I left from those days feeling more excited about the possibilities of doing ministry together and a renewed commitment to reaching out to my fellow priests here in the diocese. As a member of the Presbyteral Council, I want us to take up this topic for further reflection with the bishop. We need a common vision and need to begin planning for some creative solutions to the problems that distance and busy-ness present to us.
Priest of the Diocese of Tulsa, Presbyteral Council Member

I've seldom been to a clergy conference during which I have been more challenged. You've given me some hope.
Priest of the Diocese of Columbus

Intentional Presbyterates I-B
Claiming Our Common Sense of Purpose as Diocesan Priests
A Retreat Model

The following retreat model is provided by the Institute for Priests and Presbyterates, a program of Saint Meinrad Seminary and School of Theology, to help create an event that will serve the needs of the presbyterate and be based on the teachings of the Church. The conferences listed in this retreat model are provided by Fr. J. Ronald Knott, Director of the Institute for Priests and Presbyterates, or speakers of your own selection.

In addition to this retreat model, a presbyteral assembly model based on this theme has also been created and is included in this book.

"Claiming Our Common Sense of Purpose as Diocesan Priests" is the first of four themes designed for building presbyteral unity:

Intentional Presbyterates II: "Honoring the Variety of Gifts within our Presbyterate" focuses on how giving fellow priests opportunities to share their gifts and talents with one another is part of the work of building presbyteral unity and constitutes part of a priest's spiritual life.

Intentional Presbyterates III: "Made Holy by Our Shared Ministry" is based on themes from *Pastores Dabo Vobis*, concentrating on how a priest's three-fold ministry is his principal means of sanctification.

Intentional Presbyterates IV: "The Asceticism of Dialogue in the Ministry of Unity" is based on a theme within Pope Paul VI's encyclical *Ecclesiam Suam* to help priests learn to speak with one another more effectively.

Shepherds of Christ's flock ought to:

(a) make the ministry given to them the principal means of their sanctification, reproducing in themselves the holiness of the

things they handle
(b) lead the Church to holiness through their own example
(c) preserve the bond of priestly fraternity
(d) find their sanctification through their attachment to, and collaboration with, their bishop.

Lumen Gentium, V

Rev. J. Ronald Knott
INSTITUTE FOR PRIESTS AND PRESBYTERATES
Retreat Director
rknott@saintmeinrad.edu
(800) 357-8477

Possible Conferences

- The Spiritual Leadership of Priests in the Universal Call to Holiness
- Stages in Spiritual Growth: Where are You and Where are the People You Lead?
- Influencing People to Move From Where They are To Deeper and Deeper Discipleship
- The Character of a Pastor in Exercising Authority
- A Spirituality for Diocesan Priests and Those Who Work With Them
- The Radical Communitarian Dimension of Ordained Ministry
- The Great Scandal of Presbyteral Polarization
- What is Required of Individual Priests for Building Presbyteral Unity?
- What is Required of Others for Building the Unity of the Presbyterate?

Additional Things to Consider

- According to Canon 245.2, "seminarians, while they are in the seminary, are to be trained to take their places in the diocesan presbyterate." Inviting them to attend could be a wonderful opportunity for "group mentoring."

- The main reason for a unified presbyterate is to offer better quality pastoral ministry to the People of God. Having this event covered in the diocesan paper, with pictures, could be an opportunity to educate the laity on the presbyterate's efforts of ongoing formation.

- Involving the laity in an evening music concert and dessert event would give them a chance to show their appreciation for the ministry of priests in a non-intrusive way.

- Because dioceses and presbyterates are different, creative additions or subtractions to this outline are encouraged.

- Planning committee questions can be addressed to Fr. Ronald Knott at rknott@saintmeinrad.edu

- If this model is used, a donation to the Saint Meinrad Institute for Priests and Presbyterates would be most welcome.

Feedback from those who have used this Retreat model

The unique perspective and emphasis you placed on unity within the presbyterate, and between the priests and their Bishop, were of particular importance to me and to my priests as we continue to strive in our priestly/ presbyteral identity. Many commented that you helped them understand the theological roots for priestly fraternity; some remarked that your talk helped them become more aware of their responsibility to care for [their] brothers in the priesthood.
Sean Cardinal O'Malley, Archbishop of Boston

What a wonderful retreat the presbyterate of the Diocese of Knoxville experienced this past week with you! ...you were right on target with what we hoped this retreat would be. You helped us to recall again that as priests we are called to be men of communion and that this call is not an option. Your leadership during our retreat was a concrete example of priesthood lived in communion
Bishop Richard F. Stika, Diocese of Knoxville

On behalf of the priests of our archdiocese I want to express our deep appreciation of the wonderful retreat you directed for us. It was very informative, most interesting and extremely encouraging and challenging. It enabled us to contextualize where we are in Church and Priesthood in Ireland today. Your approach was new, fresh and life-giving and for all of that we are deeply grateful.

Archbishop Michael Neary, Archdiocese of Tuam

Your words were well thought out and clear. Your ideas encouraged us to build fraternity in a presbyterate with increasing numbers of priests working and living alone. Finally, your humor helped to keep things from getting too heavy. Afterward, attendees remained behind for a half hour continuing at their tables the discussion you started despite the fact that fresh coffee and donuts were available in the vestibule!

Francis Cardinal George, OMI, Archdiocese of Chicago

INTENTIONAL PRESBYTERATES II
HONORING THE VARIETY OF GIFTS WITHIN OUR PRESBYTERATE
A PRESBYTERAL ASSEMBLY MODEL

The following presbyteral assembly model is provided by the Institute for Priests and Presbyterates, a program of Saint Meinrad Seminary and School of Theology, to help create an event that will serve the needs of the presbyterate and be based on the teachings of the Church. The conferences listed in this assembly model are provided by Fr. J. Ronald Knott, Director of the Institute for Priests and Presbyterates, and are designed to be given by selected priests and/or lay people of your diocese.

This model is intended to help you plan a presbyterate gathering for your diocese or archdiocese that will provide ongoing formation for all members of the presbyterate. Each gathering will be as unique as each presbyterate.

"Honoring the Variety of Gifts within Our Presbyterate" is the second of four themes designed for building presbyterates:

Intentional Presbyterates I: "Claiming Our Common Sense of Purpose as Diocesan Priests" takes up the theme that priests are not priests simply one-by-one, but serve the mission of the Church in a presbyterate in union with the bishop. This assembly model focuses on the deliberate cultivation of the unity of priests with the bishop and among themselves. Additionally, a retreat model of Intentional Presbyterates I has also been created and is included in this book.

Intentional Presbyterates III: "Made Holy by Our Shared Ministry" is based on themes from *Pastores Dabo Vobis*, concentrating on how a priest's three-fold ministry is his principal means of sanctification.

Intentional Presbyterates IV: "The Asceticism of Dialogue in the Ministry of Unity" is based on a theme within Pope Paul VI's encyclical *Ecclesiam Suam* to help priests learn to speak with one another more effectively.

Pastores Dabo Vobis

The communal dimension of our ministry demands a marked asceticism of giving brother priests the opportunity to make good use of their talents and abilities, setting aside all forms of jealousy, envy and rivalry. (#28)

All (priests) are required to make a sincere effort to live in mutual esteem, to respect others, and to hold in esteem all the positive and legitimate diversities present in the presbyterate. This too constitutes part of the priest's spiritual life and his continual practice of asceticism. (#31)

The entire People of God can and should offer precious assistance to the ongoing formation of its priests. (#78)

The Basic Plan for the Ongoing Formation of Priests (United States Conference of Catholic Bishops)

The fraternal bonds of a presbyterate are forged and deepened not only in the context of prayer and work done together but also through the informal contact that priests in a presbyterate have with one another. These become occasions of mutual recognition and support and, on occasion, of healthy challenge. Given the pace of parish life and time demands that are made on -priests, a kind of planned spontaneity may be the only way that such informal contact can be made.

Recommended Schedule

Monday

1-5 p.m.	Arrival and welcome
5 p.m.	Social
6 p.m.	Dinner
	Welcome and introductions by Archbishop/Bishop
	Prayer over meal – Archbishop/Bishop

7 p.m.   Vespers
         Sharing the Vision: "The Generosity, Competence and Challenges of Our Presbyterate"
         A panel of three priests comments on these three dimenions of the presbyterate, followed by small group discussions.

8 p.m.   Movie and Discussion: "Mass Appeal"

This 1984 movie starring Jack Lemmon is a humorous, though poignant, story of a rebellious seminarian and a seasoned pastor who teaches him about the "realities" of priesthood. In the moving finale, both men reach out to each other, providing a glimpse of the tricky way in which our lives are graced by God. Even though their two styles have been reversed since 1984, the discussion to follow can help build unity across ideological divides in a humorous way. A discussion leader and discussion questions should be selected in advance.

TUESDAY

7-8:15 a.m.   Breakfast
8:30 a.m.   Lauds
9:00 a.m.   Sharing the Wisdom: Workshops

The following are examples of workshops that could be offered. Let participants attend as many sessions as possible over the two days. Some sessions could be repeated, so more individuals could attend. The "history and culture" and "charism" sessions help the presbyterate learn more about our international priests and religious communities.

- Military Chaplaincy
- Newman Chaplaincies
- Missionary Priests from Our Diocese
- Ecumenical Ministry
- Automobile Mechanics 101
- The Church in India
- Grief and Loss in the Priesthood
- Nigerian Culture and History
- Medical Ethics
- The Basics of Self-Publishing

9:45 a.m.	Break
10:00 a.m.	Workshops:

- Ecumenical Ministry
- Salvadoran Culture and History
- National Priest Organizations
- Social Service Ministry
- The Church in Poland Today
- What I Wish I Knew Before Retirement
- Seminary Ministry: Priests Working in the Seminary

10:45 a.m.	Break
11:15 a.m.	Memorial Mass for deceased priests of the presbyterate
Noon	Lunch
1 p.m.	Free time
5:30 p.m.	Dinner
6:30 p.m.	Vespers
7:00 p.m.	Sharing the Fun: Volleyball tournament for all

This bonding experience would feature a non-threatening sports event. The twist would be that those playing could not self-select the team on which they would play. Those who cannot, or do not want to, play would be cheerleaders and fans, but all would be encouraged to attend.

8:30 p.m. Social

Wednesday

7-8:15 a.m.	Breakfast
8:30 a.m.	Lauds
9:00 a.m.	Sharing the Wisdom: Workshops

- Puerto Rican Culture and History
- African American Ministry
- Ministry to the Sick
- Ministry to Divorced Catholics
- Campus and Young Adult Ministry
- Planning Your Own Funeral

9:45 a.m.	Break
10:00 a.m.	Workshops, continued

- Vietnamese Culture and History
- Personal Finances

- Organizing Overseas Pilgrimages and Tours
- Whatever Happened to Father So-and-So?
- Charisms of Our Religious Communities: A Panel of Religious Priests
- What's Happening in the Seminary These Days: A Dialogue with a Panel of Seminarians or Those Who Work with Them

A report of dismissed and missing priests would be given by a team of those who know—vicar general, vicar for priests, personnel director, etc. Confidentiality would, of course, be observed when necessary.

10:45 a.m.	Break
11:15 a.m.	Mass
Noon	Lunch
1 p.m.	Free time
5:00 p.m.	Evening prayer
5:30 p.m.	Social
6:00 p.m.	Banquet honoring those who are celebrating anniversaries
7:45 p.m.	Sharing the Talent: Concert and dessert social

A post-dinner concert/dessert social could be hosted by parish liturgical musicians and/or priest musicians from the diocese in a "coffeehouse" arrangement.

Thursday

7-8:15 a.m.	Breakfast
8:30 a.m.	Lauds
9:00 a.m.	Plenary Session: A Report by the Bishop
10:30 a.m.	Break
11:15 a.m.	Mass; Bishop presides and preaches
Noon	Lunch and departure

Additional Things to Consider

- According to Canon 245.2, "seminarians, while they are in the seminary, are to be trained to take their places in the diocesan presbyterate." Inviting them to attend could be a wonderful opportunity for "group mentoring."

- The main reason for a unified presbyterate is to offer better quality pastoral ministry to the People of God. Having this event covered in the diocesan paper, with pictures, could be an opportunity to educate the laity on the presbyterate's efforts at ongoing formation.

- Involving the laity in an evening music concert and dessert event would give them a chance to show their appreciation for the ministry of priests in a non-intrusive way.

- Because dioceses and presbyterates are different, creative additions or subtractions to this outline are encouraged.

- Planning committee questions can be addressed to Fr. Ronald Knott at rknott@saintmeinrad.edu.

- If this model is used, a donation to the Saint Meinrad Institute for Priests and Presbyterates would be most welcome.

FEEDBACK FROM THOSE WHO HAVE USED THIS MODEL

The convocation for the Presbyterate of the Archdiocese of Indianapolis was yet another very positive and, I believe, formational and engaging experience. This is my observation as a participant. My opinion has been overwhelmingly confirmed by comments from a wide spectrum of individual priests as well.

I also believe there is evidence of a genuine desire to continue to explore and develop an intentional commitment to the unity of our presbyterate. I sense a definite positive development.

Archbishop Daniel M. Buechlein
Archdiocese of Indianapolis, Indiana

This unique and creative approach, which focused on the presbyterate learning from each other and celebrating together in prayer and social gatherings, is a great gift. The initial response of the priests to the week as well as the tone that was present make it very evident to me that you have developed a direction within the Church that will bear much fruit. The pace and content of the week were excellent, and I would not underestimate the careful planning of the core committee that built the enthusiastic reception that took place.

Archbishop Joseph E. Kurtz
Archdiocese of Louisville, Kentucky

I want to express, once again, my deep thanks for your development of the Intentional Presbyterate (models). I have personally witnessed how it has strengthened the sense of unity among our priests.

Bishop Victor Galeone
Diocese of St. Augustine, Florida

Intentional Presbyterates III
"Made Holy by Our Shared Ministry"
A Presbyteral Assembly Model

The following presbyteral assembly model is provided by the Institute for Priests and Presbyterates, a program of Saint Meinrad Seminary and School of Theology, to help create an event that will serve the needs of the presbyterate and be based on the teachings of the Church. The conferences listed in this assembly model are provided by Fr. J. Ronald Knott, Director of the Institute for Priests and Presbyterates, and are designed to be given by selected priests and lay people of your diocese.

"Made Holy by Our Shared Ministry" is the third of four themes designed for building presbyteral unity:

Intentional Presbyterates I: "Claiming Our Common Sense of Purpose as Diocesan Priests" takes up the theme that priests are not priests simply one-by-one, but serve the mission of the Church in a presbyterate in union with the bishop. This assembly model focuses on the deliberate cultivation of unity with the bishop and among his priests. Additionally, a retreat model of Intentional Presbyterates I has also been created and is included in this book.

Intentional Presbyterates II: "Honoring the Variety of Gifts within Our Presbyterate" focuses on how giving fellow priests opportunities to share their gifts and talents with one another is part of the work of building presbyteral unity and constitutes part of a priest's spiritual life.

Intentional Presbyterates IV: "The Asceticism of Dialogue in the Ministry of Unity" is based on a theme within Pope Paul VI's encyclical *Ecclesiam Suam* to help priests learn to speak with one another more effectively.

MADE HOLY BY OUR MINISTRY OF THE WORD

The priest is first of all a minister of the word of God. For this reason a priest ought to develop a great personal familiarity with the word, approaching it with a docile and prayerful heart so that it may deeply penetrate his thoughts and feelings and bring about a new outlook in him, while being aware that the words of his ministry are not "his." Precisely because he can and does evangelize, the priest ought to grow in awareness that he himself is continually in need of being evangelized.

Pastores Dabo Vobis III, 27

MADE HOLY BY OUR MINISTRY OF THE SACRAMENTS

It is above all in the celebration of the sacraments and in the celebration of the Liturgy of the Hours that the priest is called to live and witness to the deep unity between the exercise of his ministry and his spiritual life. The priest's spiritual life is built up and molded by the different characteristics and demands of each of the sacraments as he celebrates and experiences them.

Pastores Dabo Vobis III, 27

MADE HOLY BY OUR MINISTRY OF LEADERSHIP

The ability to coordinate all the gifts and charisms in the community, to discern them and put them to good use for the upbuilding of the Church in union with the bishops, demands of the priest an intense spiritual life, filled with those qualities and virtues typical of a person who "presides over" and "leads" a community.

Pastores Dabo Vobis III, 27

NOTES FOR THE PLANNING COMMITTEE

- The week should be filled with educational workshops, group experiences and the showcasing of best practices.

- Workshops should be assigned to various capable priests, seminary staff and lay leaders well in advance with clear directives.

- A variety of music and worship styles should be employed during the week at Mass and Liturgy of the Hours.

- The best preachers in the presbyterate should be identified and used throughout the week for Mass, Liturgy of the Hours and Eucharistic Holy Hour.

- The parish liturgical ministers should be invited to give a concert of sacred music, old and new.

- Targeted books should be available for sale.

Recommended Schedule

Monday

1-5 p.m.	Arrival and welcome
5 p.m.	Social
5:45 p.m.	Dinner
	Welcome and introductions by Archbishop/Bishop
	Prayer before meal by Archbishop/Bishop
7 p.m.	Vespers
	Opening Talk: "The Spirituality of a Diocesan Priest: The Deep Unity between Our Spirituality and Our Threefold Ministry"
8:30 p.m.	Movie and discussion: "Chocolat" (assign a discussion leader)

Tuesday

7-8:15 a.m.	Breakfast
8:30 a.m.	Lauds
9:00 a.m.	"Made Holy by Our Ministry of the Word": Workshops

These are examples of workshops that could be offered. The speakers can come from among the priests or from resources within the diocese and the seminary (if available). Let participants attend as many sessions as possible; repeat certain workshops, if needed.

	• Using the Pulpit for Group Spiritual Direction
	• How Lay Preaching Can Help Pastors in Their Preaching Ministry
	• Preaching the Reality of "The Evil One"
	• Building a Personal Homiletics Resource Center
	• Developing an Oral Writing Style
9:45 a.m.	Break
10:00 a.m.	"Made Holy by Our Ministry of the Word" (continued)
	• Preaching Parish Missions, Retreats and Days of Recollection
	• How to Start a Homiletics Reflection Group
	• Using the Computer for Homiletics Research
	• Developing Seasonal Homiletics Series: Priests and Deacons Together
	• Using the Pulpit for Personal Sanctification
10:45 a.m.	Break
11:15 a.m.	Memorial Mass for deceased priests of the presbyterate
12:00 p.m.	Lunch
1:00 p.m.	Eucharistic Adoration
2-5:30 p.m.	Free time
5:30 p.m.	Dinner
6:30 p.m.	Vespers
7:00 p.m.	Penance Service
8:30 p.m.	Social

WEDNESDAY

7-8:15 a.m.	Breakfast
8:30 a.m.	Lauds
9:00 a.m.	"Made Holy by Our Ministry of the Sacraments": Workshops
	• Preparing to Preside as a Spiritual Discipline
	• Organizing a Multiple Wedding Ministry
	• Doing What's in the Book Well: Excellence vs. Creativity
	• Using the Rituals for Personal Prayer
	• Organizing a Multiple Funeral Ministry
	• Doing a Better Job with the Sacrament of Reconciliation

9:45 a.m.   Break
10:00 a.m. "Made Holy by Our Ministry of Leadership": Workshops
- Rights and Duties of Pastors and Parochial Vicars in Canon Law
- Parish Communication Systems: A Checklist
- Conflict Management within the Parish
- Training Effective Lay Parish Administrators
- Resurrecting Excellence in Oneself and Others
- Management as Ministry

10:45 a.m. Break
11:15 a.m. Mass
12:00 p.m. Lunch
1 p.m. Free time
5:00 p.m. Evening prayer
5:30 p.m. Social
6:00 p.m. Banquet honoring those celebrating anniversaries
7:30 p.m. Concert and dessert social

A post-dinner concert/dessert social could be hosted by parish liturgical musicians and/or priest musicians from the diocese in a "coffeehouse" arrangement.

THURSDAY

7-8:15 a.m. Breakfast
8:30 a.m.   Lauds
9:00 a.m.   Plenary Session: A Report by the Bishop
10:30 a.m.   Break
11:15 a.m.   Mass; Bishop presides and preaches
Noon   Lunch and departure

ADDITIONAL THINGS TO CONSIDER

- According to Canon 245.2, "seminarians, while they are in the seminary, are to be trained to take their places in the diocesan presbyterate." Inviting them to attend could be a wonderful opportunity for "group mentoring."

- The main reason for a unified presbyterate is to offer better quality pastoral ministry to the People of God. Having this event covered in the diocesan paper, with pictures, could be an opportunity to educate the laity on the presbyterate's efforts of ongoing formation.

- Involving the laity in an evening music concert and dessert event would give them a chance to show their appreciation for the ministry of priests in a non-intrusive way.

- Because dioceses and presbyterates are different, creative additions or subtractions to this outline are encouraged.

- Planning committee questions can be addressed to Fr. Ronald Knott at rknott@saintmeinrad.edu.

- If this model is used, a donation to the Saint Meinrad Institute for Priests and Presbyterates would be most welcome.

FEEDBACK FROM THOSE WHO HAVE USED THIS MODEL

The Holy Spirit has certainly directed you into this critical ministry. So many of our priests approached me with words of gratitude for having you as our speaker and your choice of the theme, "Made Holy Through Our Ministry." In my fourteen years of attendance at the annual diocesan Convocation, I cannot recall receiving such a positive and grateful response about our presenter. I think I can speak for our entire Presbyterate when I express our gratitude and appreciation.

Most Reverend John M. Smith
Bishop of Trenton

The convocation for the Presbyterate of the Archdiocese of Indianapolis was yet another very positive and, I believe, formational and engaging experience. This is my observation as a participant. My opinion has been overwhelmingly confirmed by comments from a wide spectrum of individual priests as well.

I also believe there is evidence of a genuine desire to continue to explore and develop an intentional commitment to the unity of our presbyterate. I sense a definite positive development.

Most Reverend Daniel M. Buechlein, OSB
Archbishop of Indianapolis

INTENTIONAL PRESBYTERATES IV
THE ASCETICISM OF DIALOGUE IN THE MINISTRY OF UNITY — LEARNING TO TALK TO ONE ANOTHER MORE EFFECTIVELY
A PRESBYTERAL ASSEMBLY MODEL

- in our families
- in our communities
- in our parishes
- in our presbyterate
- in our Church
- in our world

The following presbyteral assembly model is provided by the Institute for Priests and Presbyterates, a program of Saint Meinrad Seminary and School of Theology, to help create an event that will serve the needs of the presbyterate and be based on the teachings of the Church. The conferences listed in this assembly model are provided by Fr. J. Ronald Knott, Director of the Institute for Priests and Presbyterates, and are designed to be given by selected priests and lay people of your diocese.

"The Asceticism of Dialogue in the Ministry of Unity" is the last of four themes designed for building presbyteral unity:

Intentional Presbyterates I: "Claiming Our Common Sense of Purpose as Diocesan Priests" takes up the theme that priests are not priests simply one-by-one, but serve the mission of the Church in a presbyterate in union with the bishop. This assembly model focuses on the deliberate cultivation of unity with the bishop and among his priests. Additionally, a retreat model of Intentional Presbyterates I has also been created and is included in this book.

Intentional Presbyterates II: "Honoring the Variety of Gifts within our Presbyterate" focuses on how giving fellow priests opportunities to share their gifts and talents with one another is part of the work of building presbyteral unity and constitutes part of a priest's spiritual life.

Intentional Presbyterates III: "Made Holy by Our Shared Ministry" is based on themes from *Pastores Dabo Vobis*, concentrating on how a priest's three-fold ministry is his principal means of sanctification.

"According to a new in-depth survey...an overwhelming majority of Americans view the erosion of civility in human reaction today as a major problem. among the many signs pointing to this steady decline are the daily occurrences of cyber bullying, online 'flaming' and nasty blog comments, the venomous bickering taking place on some reality TV shows and between TV news personalities and their guests, and the mean-spirited mudslinging among politicians and their loyal supporters.... 76% of those polled said that places of worship are "very responsible" or "somewhat responsible" for improving civility in America."

Weber Shandwick and Powell Tate in
Partnership with KRC Research

"We Catholic bishops of the United States find it appropriate to offer a reminder about the importance of civility in discourse within and outside the Church. When [civility is ignored], a disservice is done to those subjected to it, to the church community or to society at large, and ultimately to those who engage in such tactics. This happens when [people] encourage disagreements on policy to degenerate into personal hostility or when they allow the ad hominem attack to replace discussion of issues. Within the church community, this disservice occurs, above all, when not only the positions held by others are questioned, which may be legitimate, but also persons' characters and their fidelity to our common beliefs.... The ministry of unity for which we bishops...are responsible has great bearing on this matter."

Civility in Media
United States Catholic Conference of Bishops (USCCB),
June 16, 2000

POPE PAUL VI'S "ASCETICISM OF DIALOGUE"

Pope Paul VI offers a structure for dialogue in *Ecclesiam Suam*, his follow-up document to Vatican II's document of ecumenism, *Unitatis Redintegratio*. He lists his principles under what he calls "the asceticism of dialogue."

"Dialogue," he says, "is a recognized method of the apostolate. It is a way of making spiritual contact." For the focus of this presbyteral gathering, we will use three of his characteristics: (a) agreement on the essentials, (b) meekness and respect in our language and (c) consensus on non-essentials.

Recommended Schedule

Day 1: Welcome and the Bishop's Update

1-5 p.m.	Arrival and welcome
5 p.m.	Social
5:45 p.m.	Dinner
7 p.m.	Vespers (Theology Chapel)
7:30 p.m.	The bishop's update
8:30 p.m.	Social

Day 2: Agreement on the Essentials

Today, the presbyterate gets clarity on what is negotiable and what is not.

"In the case of religious belief, which is central to who we are, such debates are deeply felt and, on occasion, passionately argued. This is nothing new in the Church, as the debates recorded in the Acts of the Apostles attest. While at times such disagreements can be frustrating and hurtful, good can also come from thorough and balanced expositions of different positions, so long as the teaching of the Church on the matter being reported is clearly and fairly presented."

Civility in Media, USSCB, 2000

7-8:15 a.m.	Breakfast
8:30 a.m.	Lauds
9 a.m.	"Tradition and Traditional: Essential and Non-Essential"
9:45 a.m.	Break
10 a.m.	"The Rightful Role of Individual Conscience"
10:45 a.m.	Break
11 a.m.	Mass

12 Noon   Lunch
1 p.m.   Eucharistic Adoration
2-5:30 p.m.   Free Time
5:30 p.m.   Dinner
7 p.m.   Vespers

Day 3: Meekness and Respect in Our Language

The focus is on the avoidance of arrogance, barbed words and bitterness. Talks will concentrate on the need for individual patience with contradictions, developing an inclination toward generosity and magnanimity, and acceptance of the fact that divergent views often serve to complete each other and contain some truth.

"The means of mass communication increasingly appear to be as likely to divide people as to bring them together ... . In this situation, ... the Church provides: the offer of an alternative to the way of the world ... .

Search for the truth, report the truth, and respect the human dignity of those about whom you report, whether you find them worthy of praise or blame."

Civility in Media, USCCB, 2000

7-8:15 a.m.   Breakfast
8:30 a.m.   Lauds
9 a.m.   "The Power of Language to Heal and Hurt"
9:45 a.m.   Break
10 a.m.   "Conflict Management and People of Faith"
10:45 a.m.   Break
11 a.m.   Mass
12 Noon   Lunch
1-5 p.m.   Free Time
5 p.m.   Vespers
5:30 p.m.   Social
6 p.m.   Banquet

Day 4: Consensus on Non-Essentials

- individual non-attachment to one's own preferences and points of view

- cooperative discernment (broad consultation and individual responsibility for directions to be taken and choices made)

- universal acceptance of a workable and reasonable, even if imperfect, structure for the sake of unity

"It becomes obvious in a dialogue that there are various ways of coming to the light of faith and *it is possible to make them all converge on the same goal. However divergent these ways may be, they can serve to complete each other. They encourage us to think on different lines. They force us to go more deeply into the subject of our investigation and to find better ways of expressing ourselves. It will be a slow process of thought, but it will result in the discovery of elements of truth in the opinion of others and make us want to express our teaching with great fairness."*

Pope Paul VI, *Ecclesiam Suuam*, 83

7-8:15 a.m.	Breakfast
8:30 a.m.	Lauds
9 a.m.	"The Communal Aspect of a Priest's Promise of Obedience: Non-Attachment to Personal Preferences and Points of View"
9:45 a.m.	Break
10 a.m.	"The Spirit and Process of Coming to a Consensus"
10:45 a.m.	Break
11 a.m.	Mass
12 Noon	Lunch and Dismissal

ADDITIONAL THINGS TO CONSIDER

- According to Canon 245.2, "seminarians, while they are in the seminary, are to be trained to take their places in the diocesan presbyterate." Inviting them to attend could be a wonderful opportunity for "group mentoring."

- The main reason for a unified presbyterate is to offer better quality pastoral ministry to the People of God. Having this event covered in the diocesan paper, with pictures, could be an opportunity to educate the laity on the presbyterate's efforts of ongoing formation.

- Involving the laity in an evening music concert and dessert event would give them a chance to show their appreciation for the ministry of priests in a non-intrusive way.

- Because dioceses and presbyterates are different, creative additions or subtractions to this outline are encouraged.

- Planning committee questions can be addressed to Fr. Ronald Knott at rknott@saintmeinrad.edu.

- If this model is used, a donation to the Saint Meinrad Institute for Priests and Presbyterates would be most welcome.

Rite for Renewal of Diaconal (Transitional), Priestly and Episcopal Commitments Within a Presbyteral Convocation of Priestly Commitments

Takes place after the homily.

Invitation to Prayer

The Bishop or Archbishop, without his miter, stands and invites all to pray:

My Brothers, let us pray that the almighty Father impart his blessing and grace upon us as we minister together in the holy orders we have variously received.

Litany of the Saints

All kneel or remain standing as directed for the Litany of Saints.

Hear us, Lord our God, in your great mercy, and strengthen our resolutions to serve you together in the sacramental ministries for which we have been ordained. Weak and unworthy as we are, may we bear witness together to the love and mercy won for us by our Great High Priest, your Son our Lord Jesus Christ, who lives and reigns with you, in the unity of the Holy Spirit, God, forever and ever. Amen.

All are seated.

Renewal of Commitments

The Chair of the Presbyteral Council comes forward for the presentation of resolutions.

Prior to our receiving the Holy Orders in which we minister, we were examined on our intentions. Today we have the opportunity to acknowledge and reaffirm the same resolutions that oblige us to this day. We do so relying continually on the help of God.

Will those who have received the Order of Deacon please stand?

At ordination the transitional deacon resolves:

- to remain celibate as a sign of interior dedication to Christ for the sake of the Kingdom and in lifelong service to God and mankind.

- to discharge the office of deacon with humility and love in order to assist the bishop and the priests and to serve the people of Christ.

- to hold the mystery of faith with a clear conscience as the Apostle urges, and to proclaim this faith in word and in action as it is taught by the Gospel and the church's tradition.

- to maintain and deepen a spirit of prayer appropriate to his way of life and, in keeping with what is required of him, to celebrate faithfully the liturgy of the hours for the church and for the whole world.

- to shape his way of life always according to the example of Christ whose Body and Blood he will give to the people.

The Bishop, standing, asks of them:

Are you still so resolved?

All the deacons respond:

I am, with the help of God!

The Chair of the Presbyteral Council continues.

Will those who have received the Order of Presbyter please stand?

At ordination the presbyter resolves:

- to discharge with the help of the Holy Spirit and without fail the office of priesthood in the presbyteral order as a conscientious fellow worker with the bishops in caring for the Lord's flock.

- to celebrate the mysteries of Christ faithfully and religiously as the church has handed them down to us for the glory of God and the sanctification of Christ's people.

- to exercise the ministry of the word worthily and wisely, preaching the Gospel and explaining the Catholic faith.

- to consecrate his life to God for the salvation of his people, and to unite himself more closely every day to Christ the High Priest, who offered himself for us to the Father as a perfect sacrifice.

The Bishop asks:

Are you still so resolved?

The priests respond:

I am, with the help of God!

They are then seated.

The Chair of the Presbyteral Council continues:

Let us hear again the mandate of the Holy See by which [Father] [Bishop] or [Archbishop] _____ of _____, was named [Arch]Bishop-elect of _____.

The Vicar General reads the papal bull.

After the reading, all present say:

Thanks be to God!

Two deacons, or two other assistants, go to the bishop with the Book of the Gospels. The bishop remains seated. They open the Book of the Gospels over his head in silence.

The Chair of the Presbyteral Council continues:

At ordination the bishop resolves:

- to discharge by the grace of the Holy Spirit and to the end of his life the office the apostles entrusted to bishops, which is passed on to him by the laying on of hands.

- to be faithful and constant in proclaiming the Gospel of Christ.

- to maintain the deposit of faith, entire and incorrupt, as handed down by the apostles and professed by the church everywhere and at all times.

- to build up the church as the body of Christ and to remain united to it within the order of bishops under the authority of the successor of the apostle Peter.

- to be faithful in his obedience to the successor of the apostle Peter.

- to sustain, as a devoted father, the people of God and to guide them in the way of salvation in cooperation with the priests and deacons who share his ministry.

- to show kindness and compassion in the name of the Lord to the poor and to strangers and to all who are in need.

- to seek out, as a good shepherd, the sheep who stray and to gather them into the fold of the Lord.

- to pray for the people of God without ceasing, and to carry out the duties of one who has the fullness of the priesthood so as to afford no grounds for reproach.

Are you, [Arch]Bishop _____, still so resolved?

The Bishop or Archbishop responds:

I am, with the help of God!

Renewal of the Promise of Obedience

Beginning with deacons and continuing with the priests, all who desire to do so are invited to come forward, kneel, and renew their promises of obedience as a sign of the unity in the ministerial orders. Each in turn places his joined hands between those of the bishop and says:

I, _____, continue to promise obedience and respect to you and to your successors.

They exchange the sign of peace.

When all who wish to do so have renewed their promises of obedience, the liturgy continues with the Prayers of the Faithful.

PRAYERS

A Priest's Prayer for His Presbyterate (English)

Loving God, I ask for a special blessing on all the priests of my presbyterate.

Help us to remember always that we do not work alone, but that we are an "intimate sacramental brotherhood" under the leadership of our bishop, a ministry team for which we are all responsible.

For the sake of our unified and coherent ministry, help us to remember that the ministry we do is not just personal, but a share in our bishop's ministry. For that reason, keep us always respectful of and obedient to his leadership.

Help us to be diligent in our ministry, absorbed in it, so that our commitment may be evident and our service helpful.

Help us to take good care of ourselves and to be attentive to becoming more effective in our service.

Show us ways to encourage our brothers in the seminary, those in formation who will someday be partners with us in service to the Church. Help us to set a good example for them in all that we do.

Support our sick, retired and absent brothers with your loving care.

I ask this in the name of the Good Shepherd, Jesus Christ our Lord. Amen!

Oración del Sacerdote por Su Presbiterio (Spanish)

Padre misericordioso, te pido tu santa bendición por todos los sacerdotes de mi presbiterio.

Recuérdanos que nunca estamos solos porque junto al obispo, nuestro guía, formamos una "hermandad íntima y sacramental."

Acuérdanos que tampoco trabajamos solos sino en conjunto con nuestro obispo. Concédenos el don de respeto y obediencia a su liderazgo. Ilumínanos a comprender que este esfuerzo es por el amor de un ministerio unificado y coherente que sirva al pueblo de Dios.

Infúndenos un espíritu diligente que nos lleve a realizar acciones eficaces y productivas en nuestro quehacer pastoral.

Inspíranos a que nos cuidemos y que estemos atentos a las necesidades de nuestro ministerio. Danos sabiduría para una entrega adecuada y fructífera en nuestro pastoreo.

Muéstranos los medios para animar a nuestros seminaristas, nuestros hermanos en formación, con quienes, algún día, seremos compañeros de fe al servicio de la iglesia. Ayúdanos para que les demos un buen ejemplo de conducta.

Protege y llena de amor a todos nuestros sacerdotes enfermos, jubilados o ausentes.

Todo esto te lo pido en nombre del gran pastor de almas, Jesucristo, nuestro Señor. Amén.

A Seminarian's Prayer for His Presbyterate (English)

Loving God, I ask for a special blessing on
all the priests of my diocesan presbyterate.

Help them to remember always that they do not work alone,
but that they are an "intimate sacramental brotherhood"
under the leadership of our bishop,
a ministry team for which they are all responsible.

For the sake of their unified and coherent ministry,
help them to remember that the ministry they do is not
theirs alone, but a share in our bishop's ministry.

For that reason, keep them always respectful of
and obedient to his leadership.

Help them to be diligent in their ministry, absorbed in it, so that
their commitment may be evident and their service helpful.

Inspire them to take good care of themselves and help them be
attentive to becoming more effective in their service.

Show me, and my brothers in formation, ways to encourage
our priests, those with whom we will someday be partners
in service to the Church. Help them to set a good example
for us in all that they do.

Support our sick, retired and absent priests with your loving care.

I ask this in the name of the Good Shepherd,
Jesus Christ our Lord. Amen!

Oración del Seminarista por Su Presbitereo (Spanish)

Padre misericordioso, te pido tu santa bendición
por todos los sacerdotes de mi presbiterio.

Recuérdales que nunca están solos porque junto al obispo,
su guía, forman una "hermandad íntima y sacramental."

Acuérdales que tampoco trabajan solos sino en conjunto con su obispo. Concédeles el don de respeto y obediencia a su liderazgo. Ilumínalos a comprender que este esfuerzo es por el amor de un ministerio unificado y coherente que sirva al pueblo de Dios.

Infúndeles un espíritu diligente que los lleve a realizar acciones eficaces y productivas en su quehacer pastoral.

Inspíralos a que se cuiden y que estén atentos a las
necesidades de su ministerio. Dales sabiduría
para una entrega adecuada y fructífera en su pastoreo.

Muéstranos, a mí y a mis hermanos en formación, medios para animar a nuestros sacerdotes con quienes, algún día, seremos compañeros de fe al servicio de la iglesia. Ayúdalos para que nos den buen ejemplo de conducta.

Protege y llena de amor a todos nuestros
sacerdotes enfermos, jubilados o ausentes.

Todo esto te lo pido en nombre del gran pastor
de almas, Jesucristo nuestro Señor. Amén.

A Catholic's Prayer for the Priests of the Diocese (English)

Loving God, I ask for a special blessing on
all the priests of my diocesan presbyterate.

Help them to remember always that they do not work alone,
but that they are an "intimate sacramental brotherhood"
under the leadership of our bishop, a ministry team
for which they are all responsible.

For the sake of their unified and coherent ministry,
help them to remember that the ministry they do is
not theirs alone, but a share in our bishop's ministry.

For that reason, keep them always respectful of
and obedient to his leadership.

Help them to be diligent in their ministry, absorbed in it, so that
their commitment may be evident and their service helpful.

Inspire them to take good care of themselves and help them be
attentive to becoming more effective in their service.

Show my fellow Catholics and me ways to encourage our
priests — those who offer priestly service to us in the Church.
Help them to set a good example for us in all that they do.

Support our sick, retired and absent priests with your loving care.

I ask this in the name of the Good Shepherd,
Jesus Christ our Lord. Amen!

Oración del Pueblo Santo de Dios por los Sacerdotes de Su Diocesis (Spanish)

Amoroso y Eterno Padre, te pido que bendigas a
todos los sacerdotes, de manera especial a aquellos
que pertenecen a mi presbiterio diocesano.

Ayúdalos a recordar que no trabajan solos sino que,
viven y trabajan unidos en una "fraternidad intima y
sacramental" bajo el liderazgo de nuestro obispo,
un equipo ministerial del cual todos somos responsables.

Por la unidad y coherencia de su ministerio, ayúdalos a
recordar que ese ministerio no es solamente suyo sino que,
es algo que comparten con nuestro obispo. Por esa razón,
ayúdalos a permanecer siempre unidos, respetuosos y
obedientes al liderazgo y autoridad de nuestro obispo.

Ayúdalos a ser diligentes y estregados a su ministerio para que,
su compromiso sea evidente y su servicio ayude a los demás,
de manera especial a los más marginados.

Inspíralos a que cuiden de su persona y ayúdalos a ser
eficientes en el ministerio que les has encomendado.

Enséñanos, a mí y a mis hermanos, a encontrar maneras
de apoyar a nuestros sacerdotes, quienes ofrecen su
servicio en nuestra Iglesia. Ayúdalos a que sean
un buen ejemplo para nosotros en todo lo que hagan.

Con tu amor y tierno cuidado, ayuda y consuela a
nuestros sacerdotes enfermos y jubilados, así como
también a aquellos lejos de nuestra diócesis.

Muéstrales tu rostro maternal y encomiéndalos al cuidado y
protección de María nuestra buena y santa Madre.

Te pido esto en el nombre de nuestro Buen Pastor,
Jesucristo nuestro Señor. Amén.

Discussion Questions for Various Groups within the Presbyterate

Priests Ordained More Than 30 Years

- Did you get any training in the seminary in presbyteral theology?

- Were you instructed in expectations of presbyteral members by the bishop at the time of your ordination? Would it have helped?

- How has the presbyterate changed in your lifetime? What was lost?

- What things are better than in the past when it comes to being a member of the presbyterate?

- Did you get any training in the promise of obedience? If you did, did it include the "communitarian aspect" that Pope John Paul II talked about, or was it presented as merely something between you and the bishop?

- What do you think of the ideological differences between the age groups of priests? Do you feel comfortable with some of the more recent ideological perspectives? Why or why not?

- Do you have any suggestions on how to bridge the differences, if there are some in your diocese?

- How do you feel about resigned and dismissed priests? Do you think they were treated fairly? If not, what should have been done?

- Do you look forward to retirement? Why or why not?

- What one recommendation would you make to the bishop to help unify the presbyterate more?

Priests Ordained 11-29 Years

- Did you get any training in the seminary in presbyteral theology?

- Were you instructed in expectations of presbyteral members by the bishop at the time? Would it have helped?

- Did you get any training in the promise of obedience? If you did, did it include the "communitarian aspect" that Pope John Paul II talked about, or was it presented as merely something between you and the bishop?

- Is your age group affected by ideological differences? How does your age group view this phenomenon, and do you have any ideas on how to heal these divisions?

- What do you most worry about in the years ahead?

- What could be done to help priests in your age group to face the future? By you? By others?

- Do you think resigned and dismissed priests were treated fairly? What could have been done better? Can anything be done now to reach out to them?

- What one recommendation would you make to the bishop to help unify the presbyterate more?

Priests Ordained 10 Years or Less

- Did you get any training in the seminary in presbyteral theology?

- Canon Law 245.2 (1983) says that you should have been trained to take your place in your presbyterate while you were in the seminary. Was there a concerted effort to invite you to presbyteral functions while you were a seminarian? If so, how? If not, why not?

- Would it have helped? If so, in what way? If not, would have it made the transition smoother for you? In what way? What was helpful, and what would have made it better?

- Were you prepared for the various ideological points of view in your presbyterate?

- What was your training in the promise of obedience? Did this training include what Pope John Paul II called "a communitarian aspect," or did it concern itself with just you and the bishop?

- What two issues do you think are the biggest problems for your age group relative to being a presbyteral member?

- Did you know that 10%-15% of priests nationally in their first five years leave the priesthood because of loneliness? Has this been an issue with priests leaving that you have known?

- Would a closer presbyterate have any bearing?

- What one recommendation would you make to the bishop to help unify the presbyterate more?

INTERNATIONAL AND RELIGIOUS ORDER PRIESTS

- Describe your reception into this presbyterate. What worked well, and what would have made things better?

- Was there any follow-up by anyone in the diocese to see if you were doing OK or had any special needs in the months after your arrival?

- Were you given clear expectations, or were you left to figure things out mostly for yourself?

- If you are a pastor, was there any help from the diocese about the role and expectations of pastors or was it assumed that you could find out on your own?

- Are you in favor of recruiting more international and religious order priests? If so, why? If, not, why not?

- Do you think the presbyterate understands that religious priests are actually full members of the presbyterate while serving in your diocese? How could that fact be impressed on them more?

- If you are an international priest, was there any orientation of the presbyterate to your country of origin? How was that done, or how could it be done?

- As an international priest, what is the hardest thing to get used to in your presbyterate? What changes would you recommend?

- Finish this statement: "I wish …"

CHAPTER 4

VARIOUS ISSUES RELATED TO UNITY

Formation Ministry and Priesthood in a Time of Change and Renewal

Most Rev. Gerald F. Kicanas, S.T.L., Ph.D.

I have been a bishop now for 11 years and a priest nearly 40. In today's seminary jargon, I was a "lifer," having begun my preparation for the priesthood in high school. I learned a lot in the seminary from priests, religious and laity who taught me about God, introduced me to Christ, helped me to know and accept myself, and modeled for me a passionate longing to be of service to others.

I had some great teachers and formators. Father Matt Hoffman, a high school English teacher, took us on canoe trips to the Quetico National Forest that gave confidence to a shy, awkward young man who wondered whether he could make friends and get along. Father Gene Faucher, a brand new algebra teacher who seemed to be the brightest person I ever met but who, I found out later, was trying to stay two pages ahead of us. Father Gregory O'Kelly, SJ, instilled a love for the Scriptures as the rock and foundation of a future priest's life. Father Edward Fitzgerald, our philosophy prefect, whose intensity and spirituality caused panic that I could never be as holy as he was. But I sure wanted to be. And coach Tom Kleeman, who scared the life out of people like me who were not so good in sports but wished to be star material. But thanks to coach, I did get a trophy and letter jacket for basketball never having gotten off of the bench, never having played a second of floor time.

I could go on and on, but you get my message. You have no small task, and you can make a profound difference in the lives of the seminarians you serve, even though they may not tell you. Human, intellectual, spiritual and pastoral formation of seminarians does not happen from books or lectures as much as it happens from engagement with someone like you.

Since ordination in 1967, my formation for ministry has never stopped. The love and acceptance of people from my first assignment, St. Joseph Parish in Libertyville, taught me much about what people want in a priest: not a self-centered, aloof authority but someone who steps into peoples' lives, walks with them and teaches them about the Lord.

My ministry at a juvenile detention center brought me into contact with families suffering from generations of addiction and imprisonment who were trapped in a cycle of failure almost impossible to break save for the grace of God.

Years of teaching in the seminary made me want to be an even better priest. I took inspiration from the high school seminarians and theologians who were judging and assessing priesthood through the frame of their experience with me and other seminary teachers. They expected you to be a good priest and to model what they hoped to be. I knew my shortcomings and always prayed that God would work through them to do his work.

Focus of Talk

Knowing the importance of your work, I want to reflect with you this morning on some experiences I have had as a bishop in the last few years that I think have implications for seminary formation. I hope in sharing these experiences that you might garner some insight by which you can do the important work you do even better. The church and world in which your seminarians will serve as priests has changed significantly since 1967, when I was first ordained, and I suspect will continue to change. Your task, with the grace of God, is to get them ready to serve with competence, integrity and fidelity.

The first experience is speaking up in the public arena to promote life and what we value as Catholics. The second is working with priests, deacons, religious and laity in an effort to foster communion and collaboration in their ministry. The third is trying to pass on the faith in a culture and society that too often seems indifferent and even hostile to what we believe and profess. The fourth is struggling to minister in a sometimes angry and divided church. And finally, the struggle to keep a spiritual center without which everything else becomes mere play-acting.

Stand Up and Speak Up for Justice

When I came to Arizona, a border state, I had little direct experience with immigration issues, how people came to this country and their struggles. Soon after arriving in Tucson I took a trip with 40 others across the border into Mexico to visit Altar, Sonora, a small town that has become a staging area for migrants to journey north. We visited the *Casas de Huespedes* — congested, crowded rooms where migrants slept on bunk beds piled on top of one another waiting for their trek through the desert. I talked with the people in Spanish and heard their stories and dreams, saw their fears and tears. They wanted a decent way of life, a means to care for their families. They would risk dying in the desert, whatever it took, to provide for their children. If they would get caught, they would try again later.

I watched young men gathered in the town church, heads bowed, praying privately, fervently. They trusted God would see them through. They wore images depicting the Virgin of Guadalupe, the Protectress, on whom they pinned their hopes.

We traveled down a dirt road to the path that leads to Sasabe, their entrance into the Land of the Free. We watched as van after van jammed with men, women and children passed by. Some stopped, and I gave them my blessing. I broke down looking into their eyes, hearing their humble, mumbled prayers. "Dios te bendiga!" they would say, and I would respond, "Igualemente!" And they were off, some never to make it.

I came home late that night with a different understanding of what it means to be a bishop, a priest.

Recently, I visited India and Nepal as part of a fact-finding mission for the bishops' conference to learn the state of refugees there, to understand the evil of human trafficking for sex and labor so prominent in the region, and to consider ways to help in the settlement of unaccompanied minors. I had never been to this region of the world before. While I read and studied what I might experience, it was impossible to imagine the poverty, suffering and struggle these people face every day.

Over the 10 days I could only marvel at the work of the church and priests like Father José Mathew; Father Silas Bogati; Msgr. Anthony Sharma, SJ; and Father Varkey Perekkat, SJ. They lived with the poor, stood by them, spoke up for them, nourished them with the sacraments.

Father José Mathew runs a shelter for street children whom they meet in the railroad and bus stations of New Delhi. The Salesian priests care for them, educate them, struggle to free them from their addictions. I never saw bigger smiles as the boys welcomed us and told us the agony of their ordeal and the gratitude they had for the work of this priest.

Father Silas Bogati is a diocesan priest, director of Caritas Nepal, who, despite being in a country with not one Catholic diocese and only 7,000 Catholics, accomplishes great good. He moves around on his motorcycle from one place to another, offering assistance and hope where countless people live in abject poverty.

Msgr. Anthony Sharma, SJ, vicar of Nepal, spoke with such pride as he showed us the school they have in Kathmandu, Nepal, for street children. He brought the kids to school on a day off just so we could meet them and see them perform for us. They sang and danced with much pride. They were great.

Father Varkey Perekkat, SJ, works in the Bhutanese refugee camps in Damak, Nepal. There are seven camps with 107,000 refugees who have endured this confinement for 17 years. We visited some of the English schools the Catholic Church runs thanks to Catholic Relief Services and Caritas Nepal. In one school, 1,000 children stood in front of me dressed sharply and listening attentively. They sang with pride the Bhutanese national anthem and prayed, as Hindus, to the Goddess of Knowledge. These children were born in these camps; they have known no other life. But they were not sad or sullen, but hopeful and eager.

One Bhutanese refugee working now for Caritas Nepal said, "We are weeping, every day, every night, we are weeping. We want to go home to Bhutan, our home, but we know it will never be possible." Meanwhile the church is present to them, helping and healing.

I returned to Tucson exhausted after an 18-hour flight but with a different understanding of what it means to be a bishop, a priest.

There is much evil in the world of this Third Millennium. Despite our fondest hopes that, surviving Y2K, we could bring about a world of prosperity and peace unheard of in any former generation, evil remains.

Today in 2006, a mere six years into the new millennium, much of what we hoped for, dreamt about, has come to naught. War still rages in so many places.

Poverty is the daily food of most. Abortions abound. Harm is still inflicted on the weakest. Threats escalate. We live in fear of flying, of taking a train, of sitting in a café, of walking down a street. Untold numbers of innocent people have lost their lives or their homes and livelihoods to natural disasters and senseless violence.

A bishop, a priest, cannot remain silent in the face of the overpowering evil that exists in our world. We need priests who see and hear the pain and the cries of the poor. We need priests who have the courage to speak up and to shout for human dignity. We need priests who are comfortable mingling with the poor, being among them, living like them.

Some people do not want priests like that. Some say the church, let alone its priests and bishops, has no place in speaking up and calling for change. "Stay in the sanctuary" is their expectation.

But consider what Pope Benedict XVI said in his first Encyclical Letter, *Deus Caritas Est:*

> The Church's deepest nature is expressed in her three-fold responsibility: of proclaiming the word of God, celebrating the sacraments, and exercising the ministry of charity. *(Deus Caritas Est,* USCCB Publication, N. 22)

> Our times call for a new readiness to assist our neighbors in need. The Second Vatican Council had made this point very clearly: Now that, through better means of communication,

distances between peoples have been almost eliminated, charitable activity can and should embrace all people and all needs. *(Deus,* N. 30)

The Christian's program — the program of the Good Samaritan, the program of Jesus — is "a heart that sees." This heart sees where love is needed and acts accordingly. *(Deus,* N. 31b)

Seminaries need to form priests who have "hearts that see." Introduce your seminarians to the global and local struggles that strain peoples' lives. Give them a passion for the poor and a heart that aches in the face of pain. Give them convictions that move them to act without fear or intimidation in confronting evil.

Foster Communion and Collaboration

I know some priests who have no use for the laity in ministry and some laity in ministry who have no use for priests. Petty jealousies and competition sometimes are characteristics of parish staffs. Such fighting and vying destroys their effectiveness. The demands of ministry today are such that no one can go it alone. "The harvest is plentiful, but the laborers are few."

Pope Benedict XVI, in an address to the pastoral workers of the community of *Dio Padre Misericordioso* Roman Parish, said:

> I see that you really are a living parish where you all collaborate, where you bear each other's burdens — as Saint Paul says — and thus contribute to the growth of the living building of the Lord, which is the church.
>
> She is not made of material stones but of living stones, of baptized people who feel the full responsibility of the faith for others, the full joy of being baptized and knowing God in the face of Jesus. Consequently, you are striving to ensure that this parish can truly grow. (IV Sunday of Lent, 26 March, 2006)

Recently, the bishops' conference passed a document titled "Co-Workers in the Vineyard." There were certain neuralgic issues — fears — that had to be dealt with in writing the document. The first was that acknowledging, upholding and affirming the place of laity in the ministry of the church would diminish ordained priesthood. The second involved the concern that in emphasizing the role of the laity in the work of the church, the laity's role in the marketplace would be forgotten. And the third fear was that lifting up certain laity who hold leadership roles in ministry would set up an elite group apart from all the baptized.

Even in the debate for the passage of the document, these fears were reiterated, along with the concern about using the term "minister or ministry" for the laity. Such challenges were understandable, because it was critical that the document get it right, "it" being the true relationship within Catholic teaching among the priest, deacon and lay ecclesial minister.

As Cardinal Avery Dulles, SJ, said in his annual McGinley Lecture at Fordham University on March 29, 2006,

> Ours is not a time for rivalry between clergy and laity, or between lay ministers and apostles to the world, as if what was given to the one were taken away from the other. Only through cooperation among all her members can the church live up to her divine calling. Just as the eye cannot say to the ear, "I have no need of you," so the lay minister and the social reformer, the contemplative religious and the parish priest must say to each other: I need your witness and assistance to discern and live up to my own vocation in the Body of Christ. (Dulles, "Can Laity Properly Be Called Ministers," *Origins,* April 20, 2006, Vol. 35, No. 44, p. 731)

As you prepare seminarians, it is important that you get it right as well. Recent research suggests that some newly ordained priests show a decreasing interest in collaborating with laity, especially what are described as lay ecclesial ministers.

Help seminarians to know the important, irreplaceable role they play in the church. But help them never to see themselves as the church or that they alone are responsible for the mission of Christ.

They are to be co-workers with their bishop, with one another and with all those who minister in the church. Help seminarians to embrace laity in the church as a cause for rejoicing, as those eager to lend their gifts and talents to build up the church and not those to be feared or "kept in their place."

PASSING ON THE FAITH

Over the last two years I have participated in several symposia sponsored by Catholic Universities on passing on the faith. It is the great challenge of the 21st century and the thoughtfulness and insights of these gatherings that has been challenging for me and has prodded me to imagine how we could do better.

William D'Antonio, James Davidson, Dean Hoge and Mary Gautier will soon publish a book called *Catholic Laity: Their Faith and Their Church* in which they study how Catholics of the third millennium think about their faith and the church, their identity with and commitment to the church, and how these affect their views on a wide range of issues.

They divide Catholics into four generations: pre-Vatican II, Vatican II, post Vatican II and what they call millennials (those born in 1979 or later). With that frame they look at the attitudes and opinions of Catholics.

Your future priests will pastor Catholics who are very different from those I met in 1967. Pre-Vatican II Catholics (1940 or earlier) will soon pass on. Hoge predicts that the "number of Catholics with high church commitment will probably drop by as much as one third.... Future Catholics will grant less authority to church teachings and more to their own judgment." (Hoge, Unpublished manuscript, p. 220) They suggest that "most Catholics will remain Catholic ... but attend Mass less frequently." (p. 221) They will embrace "some elements as central to the faith. They see as central helping the poor, belief in creedal statements such as Jesus' resurrection from the dead, the sacraments and devotion to Mary as the Mother of God ...." (p. 221)

He concludes, "Catholics are more highly aligned with the faith than they are attached to the Church. Moreover, Catholic identity is more stable than commitment to the Church." (p. 223) "Young adult Catholics are committed to some aspects of the faith but not to others." (p. 225)

While parts of this new study are encouraging, parts of the study give pause and challenge those who will be called to pastor God's people.

How do we lead this new generation, the millennials, into the tradition we treasure as Catholics? Clearly, we believe that faith is an act of God freely, gratuitously given, never earned. We never cause faith, but we can be the instruments through which God gives grace. As the faith has been passed on to us, we long to pass it on to others.

Introduction to the Scriptures is one powerful, poignant way that the young come to know the Lord. Priests and other in ministry need to know the Scriptures, love the Scriptures, teach the Scriptures. Too often our young are being taught the Word of God in Protestant Bible classes because there are no opportunities in our parishes.

Father Michael Himes, in a talk given at Boston College as part of The Church in the 21st Century Project, suggested in keeping with Cicero and Augustine that "effective communication [of the faith] involves teaching, delighting and persuading… Pastoral zeal cannot allow the teacher of faith simply to announce the truth, for he or she wants to move the audience to love … the teacher of faith must be knowledgeable, interesting and energizing."

Find ways to energize your seminarians and excite them about handing on the faith. Encourage them to listen to peoples' struggles with the faith and to know when and how to challenge their thinking. Convince them that just telling or lecturing or pounding information into people does not inspire and is not persuasive. Clearly, people need to know what we believe, be steeped in the tradition. We left an era of catechesis when not enough information about the faith was transmitted. Steadfast, clear teaching is necessary but in itself is not sufficient to engage a generation that is not convinced.

Paul VI says it this way. "Modern man listens more willingly to witnesses than to teachers. If he does listen to teachers it is because they are witnesses" (Paul VI, *Evangelii Nuntiandi*, N. 41).

AN ANGRY, DIVIDED CHURCH

Like you, I get lots of mail and even more e-mails. While on occasion I read a compliment or affirmation of a priest or something happening in a parish or the diocese, the vast majority of correspondence contains complaints and criticisms — people expressing upset with something happening or not being done.

I hear division and competing perspectives within parish staffs and among parishes. The comments range from "this priest is rigid, unbending, out of touch" to "this priest is not following the Church's teachings or rubrics. He does his own thing."

Today some might say that there is no one Catholic faith but different faiths, each defining Catholic by who they are with little tolerance for any different perspective. People within the household of faith can stay within a narrow circle of conversation partners and see themselves as the "true" Catholic, the one that upholds the faith.

I meet a lot of angry people — road rage is not confined to the highways. That anger can eat away at the fabric of the Church and become highly destructive.

It is important that the priests you certify for ordination be firmly grounded in the faith, strong and courageous in their commitment. But challenge them not to be self-righteous, strident or lacking in civility.

Encourage seminarians to read widely and to listen to the broad range of Catholic thought. Help them to understand that people think, act and feel differently about many things. That has always been a part of being Catholic.

Clearly, they cannot agree with or condone everything that is said and done. Schism and heresy continue to haunt the church. But they can resist adding further to dividing the household of God. They can resist setting people against one another or deliberately dividing the presbyterate. Their task is to find ways to hold the body of Christ together — unity in diversity.

Children in Nepal play a board game called "tigers and goats." Two sides vie with one another to win. Life in the church is not about taking sides, being pitted against one another, but about joining together to confront and transform a world aching to know Christ.

Spiritual Center

The Congregation for the Clergy published a document called *The Priest and the Third Christian Millennium: Teacher of the Word, Minister of the Sacraments and Leader of the Community* (Vatican City, 1999). The document concludes with a quote from *Pastores Dabo Vobis*: "New evangelization needs new evangelizers, and these are priests who are serious about living their priesthood as a specific path toward holiness" (John Paul II, *Pastores*, n. 82).

The document continues, "To accomplish this, it is fundamentally important that every priest rediscover the absolute need for personal holiness (*Priest in the Third Millennium*, p. 40). Then it quotes St. Gregory Nazianzen: "Before purifying others they must purify themselves; to instruct others they must be instructed; they have to become light in order to illuminate; and become close to God in order to bring others closer to Him; they have to be sanctified in order to sanctify" (*Orationes* 2, 71).

I have learned this in my own ministry, painfully at times. We cannot call others into the race unless we ourselves are running in it. We cannot as priests sit on the sideline cheering others on to holiness, but have to be in the pack of runners in pursuit of the imperishable prize, sometimes in the lead, sometimes in the bunch, and sometimes even trailing behind.

Every document on priesthood, every seminary rule of life, every first Mass homily speaks of the pre-eminence of sanctity and holiness in a priest's life.

Seminaries can take good men and educate them to be competent theologians and train pastoral leaders with highly honed skills.

But if the men you are educating and training are not men of prayer in love with the Lord on their ordination day and every day afterwards, you will have failed in your mission.

Recently Duke University, under the leadership of professor emeritus Dr. Jackson Carroll, completed a multi-year set of studies on pastoral leadership across denominations. The studies are titled "Pulpit and Pew" (www.pulpitandpew.edu). The astounding thing in reading these studies is how pastoral leaders seldom spoke of their own spiritual journeys or their personal prayer lives. It was not central to their reflections on their lives as pastoral leaders.

I know how hard it is for priests — and for me — to step away from the work demands to spend a day or even an hour in prayer. When asked "How are you doing personally and spiritually?" priests often respond with vague comments lacking in conviction.

In the seminary, students do pray. They celebrate the Liturgy of the Hours. They see their spiritual directors regularly and they read spiritual books. They make retreats and participate in days of renewal. They spend time before the Blessed Sacrament. They often see their own growth in holiness as central and as a first priority.

In working with priests in many different circumstances I have come to realize that that centrality and priority is not sustained in the lives of many of our priests. One of the greatest challenges to any academic institution is to teach in a way that instills lifelong learning. While I do not have specific answers to the dilemma of how to transfer a spiritual hunger to our seminarians and sustain it through their lives of ministry, I know it is crucial that it be done.

My encouragement is that you wrestle with this challenge; learn what might help from your alumni. We all know the priority and importance of stirring in our seminarians a longing for holiness.

Conclusion

You work mighty hard. You keep trying to do the best you can in preparing the next generation of priests. More than anything else I want to say how grateful I am, and I know I speak for many of my brother bishops.

I humbly offer these few suggestions:

- Instill courage to speak up for life, for peace and for justice.
- Encourage collaboration to form co-workers in the vineyard.
- Foster creativity in realizing a new evangelization.
- Form pastoral leaders who unify and do not divide.
- And above all, center all you do in leading seminarians to a lifelong journey of getting to know the Lord.

Mary, Mother of the church, pray for seminarians and priests.

Most Rev. Gerald F. Kicanas, S.T.L., Ph.D., is the bishop of Tucson, Arizona.

Reprinted with permission from the NCEA Seminary Department. This article first appeared in Seminary Journal, Volume 12, No.3 (Winter 2006).

TEACHING SPIRITUAL LEADERSHIP

Rev. J. Ronald Knott

The only priest I knew as a child, growing up in a rural parish, was Father Felix J. Johnson. He was your quintessential 1950s country pastor. Father Johnson was a real shepherd, as well as a figurative one.

Our parish property was divided in two by the main highway. On one side of the road were the church, rectory and school. On the other side was the parish cemetery. I can still remember regularly seeing Father Johnson, dressed in coveralls and carrying buckets of feed, walking through the cemetery with his sheep following him in anticipation of their next meal.

Father Johnson was a practical man, a "hands-on" kind of pastor. His sheep kept the cemetery mowed clean, and his spring lambs were one of the main entrées at our parish picnic during the summer.

Father Johnson not only designed the school, convent, rectory and parish hall himself, he also laid the bricks on all of them personally. He kept the parish books, maintained the boiler and raised his own vegetable garden. In short, he basically ran the parish by himself.

As hardworking as he was, Father Johnson did not like people all that much. He rushed through Masses and routinely snapped at people during confessions, weddings and baptisms. He had a love-hate relationship with the teaching sisters and went to as few diocesan meetings as possible. As the first seminarian from our parish in 20 years, his last words to me when I went off to the seminary at age 13 were, "You won't last till Christmas!"

I am sure he was a holy priest, at least we considered him so, but he was seriously lacking when it came to the skills of being an effective spiritual leader. He hated to preach and avoided it most of the time.

His worst nightmare was to sit down and do anything that smelled of personal spiritual direction. "Go home and say a Rosary" was his answer to every problem presented to him, whether it was spiritual or relational. He was better at giving advice on where to drill a well, as he actually did for my dad.

The real spiritual leaders of the parish were the teaching sisters. They taught us about God and how to pray. They prepared us for the celebration of the sacraments. There always seemed to be a steady stream of people going in and out of the convent after school hours. People were afraid to "ask father" so they "asked sister" to "ask father" for them.

If Father Johnson were alive today, with all the talk about giving the management functions of the parish to the laity, I am sure he would be one lost soul. He would not know what to do with himself. He was definitely a priest for his own time.

As a former pastor of four parishes myself, I think of him often, especially in my work of preparing pastors for the future.

In our Institute for Priests and Presbyterates at Saint Meinrad School of Theology, we are scrambling to catch up with the reality that our graduates will be facing immediately after their ordinations. Some will become pastors immediately, and some of them will become pastors of multiple parishes all at once.

While we are doing what we can to prepare them to work with the laity in managing their parishes, what worries me most is what we are not doing to prepare them to be spiritual leaders. Giving away the management functions of a parish does not mean that these young priests will automatically be left with incredible spiritual leadership skills. Just as in the past, it is much easier to build a gym than it is to move a congregation toward deeper discipleship.

Seminaries are doing a great job in the area of personal spirituality — better than what was being offered in my own time in the same seminary — but being holy priests will not be enough. To be effective pastors, priests today also must have the skills to lead others to holiness.

Overnight, new priests move from being recipients of spiritual formation to directing the spiritual formation of others, individuals as well as communities. Unfortunately, spiritual leadership skills are neither being taught adequately in the seminary nor being infused at ordination. A designated spiritual leader is not necessarily a real spiritual leader. Pastors of the future must not only be good personally, they must also be good at spiritual leadership. The thing that we hear most of all from the laity, when they speak at the presbyteral assemblies we are piloting through our Institute, is that they want their priests to be competent spiritual leaders.

If more than personal piety is needed by tomorrow's pastors, what then is "spiritual leadership?" From all that I have read and from all that I have learned from my own experience as a pastor, I would say that spiritual leadership is influence, the ability of one person to influence others, through invitation, persuasion and example, to move from where they are to where God wants them to be. The priest is a bridge to God and never, God forbid, an obstacle to God.

Spiritual leadership is a call from God. Therefore, real spiritual leadership must be conducted in a self-effacing, encouraging, quiet, unobtrusive, sympathetic and merciful way. A real spiritual leader lives the words written about Jesus: "A bruised reed he will not break, and a smoldering wick he will not snuff out." A true spiritual leader never gives in to pessimism and hopelessness, because he knows that God has already seen to it that the end will be victorious.

True spiritual leaders never abandon those they lead because they refuse to follow or blame them when they do not do the things they should. Rather, effective spiritual leaders step back and work on their skills to influence, induce and mobilize. Good intentions are not enough. The true test of leadership is whether people follow. Ranting and raving about how one ought to be listened to is a sure sign that one is no longer leading spiritually.

A true leader can handle rejection. Rejection can be a sign that the leader is on the right path, but it can also be a sign of serious personality defects. True spiritual leaders are honest with themselves and welcome the honest feedback of others. It is the only way to grow in spiritual leadership ability.

In parish ministry, the personal holiness of a spiritual leader is not enough, but spiritual leadership is impossible without it. What seminaries are doing in the area of personal spirituality is to be commended, but they need to be challenged to include spiritual leadership training into their spiritual formation programs if they hope to form effective spiritual leaders, as well as holy priests.

If there is a pressing need for future pastors to be spiritual leaders and it is the seminary's job to begin the process of equipping them, there are two essential questions left to explore. Can spiritual leadership be taught, and if so, how? What is best taught during the initial formation of the seminary, and what is best taught during ongoing formation after seminary?

Spiritual leadership is both a gift from God and a skill to be honed. Even if it cannot be taught like a church history class, it can be modeled, studied and emulated. In the seminary, there should be regular exposure to the great spiritual leaders of our church's long history as well as to the spiritual leaders of other faith communities — an in-depth study of how the great spiritual leaders of the past did what they did. This richer vision of spiritual formation should necessarily include witness talks from those who are leading effectively in our own day. It is helpful to study success stories.

The platforms on which the spiritual leadership of a diocesan priest is practiced are the pulpit, the presider's chair and the designated leadership role given to him by his bishop. Diocesan priests are preachers of the Word, presiders at the celebration of the sacraments and leaders of faith communities. They cannot be effective spiritual leaders without honing these three skills specifically.

Parish preaching has been called "group spiritual direction from the pulpit." Homiletics has greatly improved in seminaries, but more work needs to be done in teaching these young, busy pastors how to organize their homiletic work within a busy schedule.

"Wallowing in the Word," in preparation to preach, must become the foundation of a diocesan priest's spirituality, not just one of a hundred good things that need to be done.

Preaching and presiding at the celebration of the sacraments are one and the same: proclamation of Good News. Both are invitations seeking a response. In the Vatican II church, at long last, they have been wedded like never before. Therefore, a priest who wants to be an effective spiritual leader must know the Sacramentary and rituals from top to bottom. Studying them is a source of continuous personal spiritual growth; they are sacred tools to lead others to holiness. Familiarizing oneself with these tools before presiding at the celebration of the sacraments is an essential step in effective spiritual leadership.

Priests act *in persona Christi* in spite of their own personal weaknesses. Even though the message does not depend on the goodness of the messenger, presiders must continuously hone their skills. Of special importance is the capacity to relate to others so as to be a "bridge" for communicating Jesus Christ. This is the purpose of human formation that begins in the seminary. Likewise, a high standard of ceremony and liturgical celebration, free from spectacle and personal tastes for styles foreign to the church, must be taught and embraced, beginning in the seminary.

Some priests could be more effective. There is a world of difference between being a priest and priesting, just as there is a difference between being a designated leader and being a real leader. The seminary process is often focused on getting ordained. The question that every priest-to-be needs to ask himself, especially at the end, is this: "Now that I will be a priest, what kind of priest do I will to be?" A priest must priest and do it well!

Seminary is not enough; maybe it has never been, but this observation is certainly true these days. Long-term preparation for ongoing formation, both awakening a desire for it and seeing its necessity, should take place in the seminary. After seminary, it needs to continue for the rest of a priest's life.

Ongoing formation is an intrinsic requirement of the gift and sacramental ministry received. It is the bishop who must see to it that appropriate conditions for its realization are ensured and that his priests take advantage of those opportunities. Excellent spiritual leadership requires it.

Mother Teresa may have put the requirements of spiritual leadership simply when she said, "To keep a lamp burning you have to keep putting oil in it."

Reprinted with permission from the NCEA Seminary Department. This article first appeared in Seminary Journal, Volume 13, No. 1 (Spring 2007).

Role of the Bishop in Cultivating and Sustaining a Commitment to Lifelong Learning and Ongoing Formation within the Presbyterate

Most Rev. Joseph E. Kurtz, DD

These insights were presented as part of a panel at the Seminary Department program of the NCEA Convention on March 26, 2008, at Indianapolis, Indiana. The majority of those present were leaders involved in seminary formation.

At the invitation of Brother Bernard Stratman, SM, I am sharing insights that I presented as part of a panel that included Bishop Gettelfinger, bishop of Evansville, at the Seminary Department Program of the NCEA Convention on March 26, 2008, at Indianapolis, Indiana. The majority of those present were leaders involved in seminary formation. The title of the panel discussion was: "The Role of the Bishop in Cultivating and Sustaining a Commitment to Lifelong Learning and Ongoing Formation within the Presbyterate."

The motivation for both priest and bishop to continue formation surely flows from a commitment to continued service in and through Jesus Christ. At the Chrism Mass, the bishop asks priests if they are "ready to renew (their) own dedication to Christ as priests of his new covenant" and later beseeches the faithful to pray for him that he "may become more like our High Priest and Good Shepherd, the teacher and servant of all." Thus the task of formation seeks together to ground priestly and episcopal commitment in concrete steps. To enter into discussion on how best to do that together, I offer five points about the role of the diocesan bishop in cultivating an atmosphere within which ongoing learning and formation might thrive among priests within a diocese. I draw these observations from my eight years of experience as a bishop — first from seven years as Bishop of Knoxville in East Tennessee, and most recently for the past seven months as Archbishop of Louisville — as well as my 36 years as a priest.

The five areas for reflection are:

1. The good example of the bishop in his own ongoing formation.

2. The bishop's presence at key times in the formation of priests.

3. The development of good habits within the life of a priest.

4. Structures within a diocese to facilitate and encourage ongoing formation.

5. The type of diocesan planning and the listening required in shaping offerings.

THE GOOD EXAMPLE OF THE BISHOP IN HIS OWN ONGOING FORMATION

A few years ago I recall reading that among Americans, career enhancement is the primary driving force for continuing education. If we Americans believe we can improve our job performance, we will do almost anything, including going to seminars and reading all sorts of self-help books. As church leaders within this culture, we must assume that these attitudes also motivate us, and I can confirm that the tasks and responsibilities I have been given over the past 35 or so years have greatly influenced my ongoing formation.

There is a healthy tension between corporate offerings that bring together the entire presbyterate for ongoing formation, spiritual renewal, and fraternal support and individualized formation efforts that address gifts and challenges unique to each priest. Both are important, and one should not be short-changed for the other. In the early '70s, when Bishop McShea of Allentown invited me to prepare for the work of Catholic Charities by receiving a master's degree in social work, a field of interest was presented to me that both challenged the gifts that God gave me and prepared me for the pastoral work that would be mine. Both the challenge and the preparation were great motivators. For other priests, gifts in the areas of teaching, chaplaincy or preaching might lead in different directions.

In addition, the offerings for the total presbyterate are also opportunities that ought to be used to the full. Although some of the skills addressed through continuing formation may be geared toward a particular profession or discipline, it is my experience that these skills contribute to the total ministry of the priest, and the ministry of the priest in turn deepens and confirms these skills. For me, the ongoing formation in which a social worker or family therapist engages was a clear help in my pastoral service within the church, and my daily application of these skills in the life of the church ensured that this special ministry was the right fit. (In my fifth point I will speak of the importance of listening in diocesan planning, so that the offerings to priests can match in some fashion the pastoral questions and needs surfacing within the life of the presbyterate as well as within the diocese.)

As a bishop, I continue to see the corporate gatherings, such as the offerings of the USCCB at our regular meetings or the biannual conference on medical moral issues offered by the National Catholic Bioethics Center for Bishops, as very important in my personal formation plan. I also am pursuing an individualized plan. I have begun a monthly overnight at the hermitage in the Abbey of Our Lady of Gethsemani. At this overnight, I join the Trappists in communal prayer and engage in personal prayer and reflection. I began a book that I tend to continue to read over the coming weeks (or months, depending on my reading speed). These mutual incentives support one another. Without intending this directly, I am finding that my own efforts, imperfectly done, are an incentive to ongoing formation among our priests. My overnight with the Trappists is actually an imitation of a practice of one of our priests in Louisville. It is my hope that this example will spur others to do the same.

The Bishop's Presence at Key Times in the Formation of Priests

It does not take long for a priest to learn that the most powerful pastoral moments are often those without a word: a presence at a hospital bedside or even a school basketball game. Presence has the power to convey support and encouragement like no motivational speech can. Thus the quiet presence of the bishop, often learning along with the priests of the presbyterate, is a powerful way to promote ongoing formation.

While there are many demands on the time and energy of the bishop, I believe that active participation is much more valuable than a token visit to show support. Such active sharing in a program of priestly formation also is a goldmine for listening and uncovering new themes for future planning and support.

The Development of Good Habits within the Life of a Priest

Any worthwhile effort begins with a gift to be developed, inner discipline to develop that gift and the capacity of a community to support the expression of the gift. At confirmation Masses I often use the example of one playing the piano or being successful on the football field to illustrate those three stages. Knowing one's God-given gifts and then having the inner habits to develop these gifts are time-tested and true approaches, and of course the encore from the audience or cheers from the bleachers bring the action to a completion.

The byproduct of both is a contribution to the well being of a community, seen clearly in the accomplished pianist's building up a culture of art and in the true — if not as sublime — building of success and esprit de corps by a football player at the NFL Super Bowl.

These qualities of inner discipline must be learned.

Seminary formation, while truly building on the habits and virtues of the family and early school, is an essential time to be intentional in the development of these habits. Good study habits are well known, but such habits should include reinforcements that support a thirst for the adventure of learning and the challenge of stimulating conversations. My seminary days included not only study halls and group learning for tests but also "Great Books" seminars and the opportunity to take an occasional elective in counseling at a local university.

Structures within a Diocese to Facilitate and Encourage Ongoing Formation

When I went to Knoxville I became aware that the practice of taking a sabbatical was a policy on the books. Here in Louisville sabbaticals are integrated into the life of the presbyterate. There is a need to make this practice real by proper budgeting and by planning to assist with pastoral duties in the absence of the priest. Attention to reasons why there is not greater use of sabbaticals and other opportunities for individual formation will help in continuing to reform a diocesan structure to better facilitate formation of priests.

The Type of Diocesan Planning and the Listening Required in Shaping Offerings

Planning involves levels of careful listening. For ongoing formation to be effective there needs to be that level of listening and applying. One example of this is the listening process that I have experienced over these seven months in Louisville. I went to each of the 12 regions in which our priests and parish administrators meet to listen to the joys and challenges on the minds and in the hearts of those who work together in the regions. Not only did this process give me a great feel for the uniqueness of each region within the archdiocese, but it also identified some patterns or themes alive in the lives of our priests. My hope is that ongoing formation might seek to address some of these themes.

Father Chuck Thompson, whom I am appointing vicar general, will have special responsibility for assisting me in the life and ministry of priests. He plans on making similar visits to regional gatherings of priests and parish administrators in the coming year to ground some of these perceptions and bring them to life. Obvious themes that have come to the fore include the capacity of pastors to be effective in the administration of the parish without being overwhelmed by administrative details, the need to have healthy work relationships with a pastoral staff and the importance of healthy relationships with consultative bodies.

Another example of good listening occurred in Knoxville when I began an annual informal gathering with the help of Father Peter Iorio. Newly ordained priests, along with their pastors, gathered with me for prayer and dialogue. There is a theory of family systems that claims more limited sharing with a wider group is more valuable than full sharing in private. I found that this gathering met its potential to surface shared wisdom among the participants in the group and that it provided an important presence for me as bishop in the critical early days of a newly ordained priest. It also helped to facilitate the relationship between pastor and associate pastor, and it surfaced some "best practices" for those present while serving as a source for diocesan planning and ongoing formation topics.

In the homily at the ordination of a bishop are found these challenging words: "With the charity of a father and brother, love all whom God places in your care, especially the priests and deacons, your co-workers in the ministry of Christ." Such love and care finds expression in many ways but none more pointed than in the daily prayer of bishops for the priests (and deacons) with whom he serves and for their ongoing formation. Thus, such cultivation and sustaining of their formation is a large priority in the life of a bishop. As I hope my observations point out, living out his promise is integral to the pastoral life of a bishop and not simply an additional responsibility. In this way, we serve the people of God and, as the bishop at the Chrism Mass calls on the faithful to pray, we become "a genuine sign of Christ's loving presence" among them.

Most Rev. Joseph E. Kurtz, D.D., is the archbishop of Louisville. Previously he was bishop of Knoxville. He has a master's degree in social work and has held many positions in the field of Catholic social services.

Reprinted with permission from the NCEA Seminary Department. This article first appeared in Seminary Journal, *Volume 14, No. 2 (Fall 2008).*

CHAPTER 5

A Parable of Unity

A Parable for Presbyterates

Let a priest attract the hearts of young people to the priesthood by his own humble and energetic life, joyfully pursued, and by love for his fellow priests and brotherly collaboration with them.
Document on Priestly Formation 1, 2

The Rabbi's Gift

Anonymous

A famous monastery had fallen on hard times. Formerly its many buildings were filled with young monks, but now it was all but deserted. People no longer came there to be nourished by prayer, and only a handful of old monks shuffled through the cloisters, serving God with heavy hearts. On the edge of the monastery woods, an old rabbi had built a little hut. He would come there, from time to time, to fast and pray. No one ever spoke with him, but whenever he appeared, the word would be passed from monk to monk: "The rabbi walks in the woods." And, for as long as he was there, the monks would feel sustained by his prayerful presence.

One day the abbot decided to visit the rabbi and open his heavy heart to him. So, after the morning Eucharist, he set out through the woods. As he approached the hut, the abbot saw the rabbi standing in the doorway, as if he had been awaiting the abbot's arrival, his arms outstretched in welcome. They embraced like long-lost brothers. The two entered the hut where, in the middle of the room, stood a wooden table with the scriptures open on it. They sat for a moment in the presence of the Book.

Then the rabbi began to weep. The abbot could not contain himself. He covered his face with his hands and began to cry too. For the first time in his life, he cried his heart out. The two men sat there like lost children, filling the hut with their shared pain and tears. But soon the tears ceased and all was quiet. The rabbi lifted his head. "You and your brothers are serving God with heavy hearts," he said.

"You have come to ask a teaching of me. I will give you a teaching, but you can repeat it only once. After that, no one must ever say it aloud again."

The rabbi looked straight at the abbot and said, "The Messiah is among you." For a while, all was silent. The rabbi said, "Now you must go."

The abbot left without a word and without ever looking back. The next morning, the abbot called his monks together in the chapter room. He told them he had received a teaching from the "rabbi who walks in the woods" and that the teaching was never again to be spoken aloud. Then he looked at the group of assembled brothers and said, "The rabbi said that one of us is the Messiah." The monks were startled by this saying.

"What could it mean?" they asked themselves. "Is Brother John the Messiah? Or Brother Matthew or Brother Thomas? Am I the Messiah? What could all this mean?" They were all deeply puzzled by the rabbi's teaching, but no one ever mentioned it again. As time went by, the monks began to treat one another with a new and very special reverence. A gentle, warm-hearted concern began to grow among them that was hard to describe but easy to notice. They began to live with each other as people who had finally found the special something they were looking for, yet they prayed the Scriptures together as people who were always looking for something else.

When visitors came to the monastery they found themselves deeply moved by the lives of these monks. Word spread, and before long people were coming from far and wide to be nourished by the prayer life of the monks and to experience the loving reverence in which they held each other. Soon, other young men were asking, once again, to become a part of the community, and the community grew and prospered. In those days, the rabbi no longer walked in the woods. His hut had fallen into ruins. Yet somehow, the old monks who had taken his teaching to heart still felt sustained by his wise and prayerful presence.

LIST OF MAJOR DOCUMENTS

The Basic Plan for the Ongoing Formation of Priests, United States Catholic Conference, Inc., Washington, DC, 2001.

Christus Dominus, The Documents of Vatican II, Walter M. Abbott, S.J., General Editor.

Code of Canon Law, Canon Law Society of America, Washington, DC, 1983.

Optatam Totius, The Documents of Vatican II, Walter M. Abbott, S.J., General Editor.

Pastores Dabo Vobis, St. Paul Books & Media, Boston, MA, 1992.

Presbyterorum Ordinis, The Documents of Vatican II, Walter M. Abbott, S.J., General Editor.